The
INSIDER'S GUIDE
to Home Inspection

by
Frank Ross
with
Natalie Ross

Published by Pocket Shell Publishing

© 2016 Frank Ross with Natalie Ross

All rights reserved

No part of this book may be reproduced in any form whatsoever, whether by graphic, visual, electronic, film, microfilm, tape recording, or any other means, without prior written permission of the publisher, except in the case of brief passages embodied in critical reviews and articles.

ISBN 978-0-9971665-0-7

Published by Pocket Shell Publishing

Library of Congress 2016951086

Cover design, illustrations, and typeset by Kenyon Sharp, *www.kenyonsharp.com*

All photos or images property of Frank Ross unless otherwise noted

Printed on acid-free paper

Table of Contents

Preface i

Introduction iii

Part 1: Background and Basics

Chapter 1: Why Get a Home Inspection? 1

Chapter 2: What is a Home Inspection? 4

Chapter 3: What is an Inspector? 10

Chapter 4: What Does an Inspector Do?. 16

Chapter 5: Types of Inspections 30

Part 2: Down and Dirty

Chapter 6: Components of an Average Home 38

    Section 6.1: Electrical 38

    Section 6.2: Plumbing. 47

    Section 6.3: Heating and Cooling. 58

    Section 6.4: Structure 71

    Section 6.5: Building Envelope 82

        Roof and Attic 82

        Cladding. 101

        Windows and Doors 108

Part 3: This and That

Chapter 7: Maintenance Tips 120

    Section 7.1: Landscape and Drainage 120

    Section 7.2: Plants and the Home 122

    Section 7.3: Regular Maintenance 126

    Section 7.4: First Impressions 128

Chapter 8: Termite Facts. 131

Chapter 9: Mold Basics. 135

Chapter 10: Home Repair and Renovation 137

Chapter 11: Safety and Security 142

Chapter 12: History of the Home Inspection Report. 149

Conclusion. 152

Index 154

The Insider's Guide to Home Inspection

By Frank Ross with Natalie Ross

The one piece of advice most offered to aspiring writers is "Write what you know." Obviously it doesn't mean to literally only write what you've experienced, but to draw on your experiences. Put some of yourself into your writing so readers will be able to relate to the story. While this is not a novel, I have taken that advice to heart and written what I know, what I've seen and what I've learned. Because of that, my writing will reflect the geographical region in which I live and work. Some of what I have shared can be applied across the nation; however, other perspectives reflect, by necessity, what I know about homes in Southern Utah. Take it like a writer should take that piece of advice… use what you can and disregard the rest.

Introduction

So, you are buying a house, and you're undecided about whether you need an inspector to look at it before you seal the deal. Maybe you want to see what's involved in a home inspection because you think you might be able to handle it on your own. Or you're selling your house and you think it would be good to have an idea of what the buyer's inspector will find before he gets there. Perhaps you're a new homeowner and you're looking for helpful tips or advice on maintaining your investment. It could be you've bought the home "as-is" and you need to know how to uncover deficiencies that need your attention. No matter the reason you picked up this book, you'll find a lot of useful information between its covers.

Part 1: Background & Basics

Chapter 1: Why Get a Home Inspection?

Buying a home is one of the most significant decisions and one of the biggest investments most people will ever make The process of purchasing a home can be complicated. There are a lot of steps to complete, paperwork to fill out and sign, hoops to jump through, decisions to make, all of which can lead to a great deal of stress. Being certain that the home is in good shape should be a top priority. A professional home inspection is an evaluation of the condition of the home by a trained expert. The report should include information on all the home's major systems and various additional components - the roof, the foundation, the structural system, plumbing and electrical systems, heating and cooling system, the attic, crawlspace, major built-in appliances (when they are included with the sale), windows, doors, switches, outlets, and more.

A home is made up of more than its various components and systems. It's where quality time is spent with family and friends. It's a method of saving for the future, perhaps for retirement, or for an inheritance for the children. It's your version of the American dream come true. All these feelings and emotions impact the purchase process. Buying a home is not just a financial investment.

Budget constraints and credit scores may dictate how much a person can afford to spend, but the final decision will depend on what your heart tells you. Like falling in love – when you find the right house, it will feel like coming home.

Once emotions enter the decision-making process, many buyers may be blinded to a home's deficiencies. Undiscovered issues can result in your dream home becoming a nightmare. A professional home inspection is intended to provide buyers the opportunity to learn many essential details about their prospective home, to receive answers to important questions, and to give them peace of mind. But finding out that your desired home has defects and problems may rob you of that peace.

Remain Calm. What the inspector has to say and the findings in his report will be mostly maintenance recommendations, information on the home's systems, observations and suggestions. These comments are handy. However, the issues that really matter can be narrowed down into just a few categories.

Major defects, of course, would require consideration. An example of this would be a large section of a floor joist cut out to install bathroom plumbing. Safety hazards, also potentially major, might include missing smoke detectors, faulty GFCIs, capped off water heater pressure & relief valves. Deferred maintenance or conditions that could lead to major defects will need to be addressed as some point. A loose and leaky toilet, for example.

CHAPTER 1: WHY GET A HOME INSPECTION?

Anything falling into these categories should be discussed by the buyer and their real estate professional. Often a potentially significant problem can be remedied at very little cost with the result being greater protection to both life and property. For example, a missing stairway hand rail, or faulty GFCI receptacle may not cost much money to install or repair and may be considered "just a minor thing," but if someone were to get hurt or die from an electric shock, then that faulty GFCI receptacle could cost more than the entire house cost to buy. I recommend that the buyer consult with their real estate professional when reviewing the inspection report and then decide what they want to do about major defects, deferred maintenance items, safety issues, etc.

An inspection of the home under consideration will help home buyers make an informed decision during the purchase process. Even newly constructed homes can benefit from a professional evaluation. Equipped with a baseline on the condition of the home and sound home-maintenance information, buyers stand a far better chance of protecting their investment and increasing its value over time.

Many times homeowners are genuinely surprised to learn about defects an inspector uncovers. As a buyer, realize that the inspection report is not a to-do list for the sellers or the buyers. It is an evaluation of the home, a tool to help everyone involved to be more fully aware of the condition of the home. Every home will have deficiencies of some sort. Keep things in perspective. Use the inspection report as a guide to make conscious choices about what you can live with or repair yourself and what is unacceptable to you and needs correction. Do not walk away from your dream home over things that do not really matter.

Chapter 2: What is a Home Inspection?

Josh and Jenna were in the market to buy their first home. After a careful search of available properties, they, and their real estate agent found a home they liked. Once their offer was accepted, they scheduled a home inspection. We met at the house on a late summer afternoon. It was located in an established neighborhood, with clean, well-kept homes outlined with maturing trees and neatly-trimmed hedges. Brightly colored flowers in tidy beds dotted the yards. From the street, the house looked like most of the other homes nearby—except the garage window was broken, probably by a stray baseball.

I began by walking around the outside of the house, noting that the ground tended to slope away from the structure and the trim was freshly painted. Climbing onto the roof, I could see damage from a previous violent summer storm: an 8-inch by 4-inch spot where the wood sheathing was exposed, and a few broken tiles. I noticed that the heat pump was original, about 20 years old. A quick glance around at the neighboring roofs revealed that more than half the neighbors had already replaced similar units.

In the garage I found some concerns. A previous homeowner had cut a hole in the fire-rated door to install a pet door, probably so the litter box could be kept in the garage. Also, the cover for the attic hatch was missing. I later discovered it in the attic. And there was one double tap in the breaker panel. The wiring I could see in the panel was copper.

When I went inside, I recognized the appeal of the home to Josh and Jenna. Quiet ceiling fans rotated in each room. The kitchen had been upgraded with new appliances. New ceramic tile covered the floors throughout the home except for the bedrooms and living room. Bathroom fixtures were also new and shiny.

When I completed my inspection, I explained the inspection report to my clients. Most of the items on my list of concerns were minor such as a GFCI outlet needing to be installed in the kitchen, and a leak under the island sink. I also reported that the weatherstripping around the front door may need to be replaced and that the master bedroom door wouldn't latch.

As I finished, Jenna was beaming. "We can handle this stuff!" she said. "I'm so glad to know we're not going to be broke and always worried about what's going to go wrong next."

Two real estate agents stopped by at that moment with clients in tow. "Sorry," Josh told them, "This home is sold."

Buying a home can be a nerve-wracking process. There are a multitude of details requiring a buyer's attention. Having a clear picture of the condition of the home to be purchased helps a buyer make educated decisions.

According to the Department of Housing and Urban Development a home inspection is an evaluation of a home's condition by a trained expert. During a home inspection, a qualified inspector takes an in-depth and impartial look at the property his client plans to buy.

Even with all the apparent advantages to having an independent and experienced set of eyes look over a homebuyer's potential new home, a lot of people still choose to forego the home inspection. Many times this choice is based on a misconception, such as those described in the following list of common myths regarding home inspection and inspectors.

Myth 1: Home inspectors are all the same so it doesn't matter who I choose.

Truth: Currently only about half of all states have any licensing requirements for home inspectors. Each home inspector comes with his own unique background, skill set, and professional training. They are not all the same. A couple of words of advice on finding a good inspector would be to first find out if your potential inspector is part of a professional organization. The top three organizations for home inspectors are the American Society of Home Inspectors (ASHI, found online at *www.ashi.org*), the National Association of Home Inspectors (NAHI, online at *www.nahi.org*) and the International Association of Certified Home Inspectors (InterNACHI, *www.nachi.org*). Another good way of gauging the inspector's experience is to ask him how many inspections he does each year. A good number is a minimum of 200. Any amount less than that and he is probably doing inspections only part-time and may not be keeping up to date with the profession the same way a full-time inspector would.

Myth 2: There is no point in getting a home inspection if the home is being sold "as-is."

Truth: Actually, when a home is being sold "as-is" it is more important than ever to have an inspection performed. When no seller's disclosure is being provided or when a number of problems are apparent, a wise buyer should have another pair of eyes looking over the property. The home inspection report will provide a greater understanding of the condition of the home and provide more information that the buyer can use to decide whether or not to proceed with the purchase and negotiate price.

Myth 3: A termite inspection or appraisal as required by the lender is all that is needed.

Truth: A home inspection fills a different purpose than the termite inspection or the appraisal. The termite inspection, as the name implies, is targeted toward finding termites or other wood destroying organisms in the home. It's focus is too narrow to include all the home's systems. The appraisal is a tool used by the lender to help determine the value of the home for lending purposes. While some of what the appraiser reports on pertains to the condition of the home, his purpose in looking at it is very different than the home inspector.

Myth 4: Newly built homes don't need to have an inspection.

Truth: Skipping the inspection on a newly built home could be one of the costliest myths of all. Builders are human too and they sometimes make mistakes. Personally, I have found patio doors with cracked glass, a granite bar top not properly supported, the stucco weep screed (intended to drain moisture from the wall system) covered with soil, and one home with several of the windows installed inside out. In another home, the installer had left the instruction manual on the burners inside the furnace. Another home was a year old, but had never been lived in had air conditioning units on site that had never been connected.

Myth 5: An inspector referred by the real estate agent will favor the agent.

Truth: Some clients will worry if the home inspector and the agent seem to know one another. The truth is that the home inspector works for the buyer when doing a pre-purchase home inspection. Sometimes the inspector's findings will cause the buyer to reconsider his offer to purchase. And when the deal falls through like that, some agents are not too happy with the inspector. An inspector can't let that possibility influence his report, however, because his job is to do the best he can for his client, the buyer.

Myth 6: The inspector will uncover all the problems in the home.

Truth: It is just not reasonable to expect that the home inspector can find ALL the problems in a home in the limited amount of time he has to spend there. Instead, his report will reflect the condition of the home at the time of the inspection. He will test the home's systems, look at the structure and try to uncover any potential pitfalls, recommending further evaluation by a specialist when needed. His goal is to provide the buyer with a further body of information upon which to make their decision. Undoubtedly, in some cases, defects will show up later.

CHAPTER 2: WHAT IS A HOME INSPECTION?

For example, a house inspected on a bright, sunny autumn afternoon may not show a window frame leaking until the first spring rain storms beat on it. There is no way the inspector could have found that when he was there. And, really, those kinds of situations are just a normal part of owning a home.

Buying a home is never easy. Owning a home is never easy. But buying a home that has been inspected by a professional, independent inspector can make home ownership much easier. The inspection report should be referred to when making home improvements, remodeling, or adding on to the home. It can help you budget for replacement of components that may be nearing their life expectancy. And, like it did for Josh and Jenna, it can give you valuable peace of mind about the biggest investment of your life.

Chapter 3: What Is an Inspector?

One day I inspected a home at which the buyer was present. I had been at it for about thirty minutes when the home buyer asked me, "Well, what do you think the home is worth?" I replied, "I have no idea. I do not get involved with the value of a home." He came back with, "Aren't you an appraiser?" "No," I responded, "I am a home inspector." "Well, what does a home inspector do?" he asked. So I proceeded to educate him on the differences between an appraiser and a home inspector.

An appraiser provides an appraisal report stating his professional opinion of the estimated value of a property.

A home inspector has nothing to do with the value of a home and he should not even attempt to answer the questions, "Do you think this is a good buy?" or "Do you think I should buy this home?" Instead, he provides a report of the condition of the home at the time he is there, which the buyer can then use as a tool to help him decide whether or not to purchase the property.

A home inspector will check the operation of the plumbing system which includes the fixtures in bathrooms and the kitchen, the laundry room, hose bibs, water heater, and more. He will also check the roof, attic, crawlspace, exterior of the home, the lay of the land as it relates to water drainage, concrete walks and driveways, the electrical system, doors, windows, locks, lights, receptacles, foundation, walls, floors, ceilings, fans, attic ventilation, and the cooling and heating systems. He will look for safety concerns such as defective GFCIs, faulty AFCIs, garage doors that don't reverse, problems with the door to the garage from the home, unsafe stairs, missing or inappropriate hand rails or guard rails, any tripping hazards, and other items like these.

The home inspector has all loyalty to his client and won't discuss the report with the home owner unless there is a safety concern for life and/or property. For example one time as I was taking out a screw that holds the electrical panel cover to the wall, I was startled by sparks flying from the panel. I stopped then and there and told the home owner she needed to get an electrician out to the home as soon as possible to pull the panel and see what was wrong. Another example would be if I were to find an active water leak in some out of the way place such as under a house where perhaps a sink drain pipe has come apart or a water line is leaking badly. I would tell the home owner about it so they can get a plumber to their home without delay.

A home inspector does not give a guarantee on the home. This is just not possible. The report is an evaluation of the home at the time of the inspection as well as the home inspector's opinion of things he has found. True, one home inspector may find and write up something that another home inspector will not mention in his report. This does not mean that the one inspector missed the item. Instead it may mean that one inspector may be too picky, or it may mean that the other inspector does not consider an item found to be significant enough to mention in his report.

One day I was setting up my equipment at a home preparing for the home inspection when the woman buying the home, my client, said, "Well, I bet you can guarantee me that you will find everything in this home." I replied, "No, but I will guarantee that I will write down everything that I do find." A home buyer should be aware that it is not uncommon for her to find something that needs to be repaired that is not in a home inspection report. A good home inspector will only be at an average size house for about three hours. During that time he will be trying to find things that may be a red flag or a safety concern to the welfare of the occupants. It is not possible for him to check each and every receptacle, light, and window. Sometimes this is due to time constraints and sometimes because of other reasons. He may not be able to access a window if, for example, there is a large TV or a dresser in the way. Standards of practice that inspectors follow do not allow him to unplug items from receptacles to test them. He is also not authorized to move furniture so it's possible for something previously hidden to show up once the home is vacant.

Every now and then clients will comment that a home inspector should be able to find everything that is wrong with the home in the short, few hours he will be inspecting the home. This expectation is just not reasonable. I can say that a home inspector will or should try to find everything he can find in the time they have to do the inspection. However, after the client moves in and spends some time in the home, they may find a cracked floor tile, a squeaking door, maybe a receptacle that was obstructed during the inspection that has no power, or some other or two.

CHAPTER 3: WHAT IS AN INSPECTOR?

A home inspector, believe it or not, is a human being, subject to making mistakes. A friend of mine who is an inspector in another state told me of a conversation between him and a friend of his who is an attorney. The attorney asked what a home inspector does, and upon hearing the answer, the attorney said that he would not touch the job of a home inspector for less than $1000 an hour because of all of the liability he takes on.

People need to understand that home inspectors are just like any other professional. They are trying to do their best. Just like doctors or auto mechanics, the longer these professionals are in business the more they will learn. They are able to take advantage of better and newer equipment that is developed. They simply get better over time, and they may be able to fix or find something today that they did not even know existed last year.

So how do you go about choosing a good home inspector? A favorite movie of mine is Armageddon starring Bruce Willis. In it, an asteroid is headed on a collision course with Earth and the only chance of survival is for oil drilling expert Harry Stamper (Willis) and his team of roughnecks to venture into space to drill a hole 800 feet deep in the asteroid. A nuclear charge will then be inserted and detonated causing the asteroid to break into two pieces, which would then each take a different course and miss hitting the earth. Just as the space shuttle is about to blast off, the genius geologist says the following, one of my favorite lines from the movie:

Rockhound: You know we're sitting on four million pounds of fuel, one nuclear weapon and a thing that has 270,000 moving parts built by the lowest bidder. Makes you feel good, doesn't it?

The National Association of Home Builders estimates that over 3,000 components are used in constructing a house. An average 2500 square foot house all on one level might have over 1550 shingles, 10 to 20 or more windows and the same number of doors, half a dozen major systems (such as heating, cooling, electrical, and plumbing), a minimum of 25 electrical outlets, half again as many light fixtures and all the structural components that hold the rest together. It's not the space shuttle, but it's complex in its own way.

The increasing demand for professional home inspections has encouraged good inspection companies to train their inspectors to perform at a high level, although licensing is still not a requirement in many states. Home inspectors need to have expertise in all the house's systems. Please be aware that all home inspectors and home inspections are NOT the same.

It's important to choose an inspector who provides a comprehensive visual inspection of a house, reporting on interior and exterior items in a comprehensive survey. Potential clients could interview inspectors to find one who is, first, highly trained to inspect all systems for existing and potential problems, and, second, follows professional standards of practice for reporting. Ask if the inspector carries errors and omissions insurance, a sign of a responsible business. Membership in a national trade organization is also a measure of credibility.

Other questions to ask include this list from the US Department of Housing and Urban Development (HUD) Federal Housing Administration:

- What does the inspection cover?
- How long have you been practicing in the home inspection

profession and how many inspections have you completed?
- Do you offer to do repairs or improvements based on the inspection?
- How long will the inspection take?
- How much will it cost?
- What type of inspection report do you provide and how long will it take to receive the report?
- Will I be able to attend the inspection?

Uncovering defects isn't the primary purpose of a home inspection. A truthful representation of the condition of the house is the main goal of the report. Most of the time my report provides support for the buyer's decision so that he or she can proceed with the next step in the purchase process with confidence. Peace of mind is a precious commodity when you are making the major purchase of your life. Will you trust the lowest bidder to provide it?

Chapter 4: What Does an Inspector Do?

One day as I met some buyers and their realtor at a home that I was going to inspect, the realtor jokingly said to the buyers, "Frank is the best there is. He will find everything that is wrong with this house." Immediately, but politely, I joined this conversation to clear up this misconception. I told the buyers and their realtor that a home inspection is a visual inspection and even though I am very thorough I cannot guarantee that I will find everything that is wrong with the home. I told them that my toolkit does not include X-Ray glasses, and so I will have to do the best that I can with what I have. That got a laugh from them but they understood that a home inspector is not Superman and cannot see through walls, roofs, or underground (relatively new to the home inspection industry are infra-red cameras. They are the closest thing to X-ray vision currently available. Basically they can detect temperature differences in walls and floors).

A home inspector will charge a certain fee to visually inspect a home. The report is a 'snapshot' in time of what he sees. In the time that he takes to inspect a home a home inspector is checking the plumbing system, heating and cooling systems, electrical system, the roof and the foundation, the attic and crawlspace, as well as any major built-in appliances. There are hundreds of different items. Only a sampling can be discussed here.

The inspector will check the plumbing distribution piping and waste piping that can be seen. The inspector will also check plumbing fixtures by operating the faucets, toilets, showers, sinks, etc., but he cannot fill tubs to capacity to see if the over flow is hooked up or leaky. He should be running the dishwasher one full cycle to see that the unit works but he cannot do a load of dishes to see how well it cleans.

The inspector will visually check the water heater for leaks, rust, corrosion, a proper relief valve installation and that the burner works properly. He does not check to see that there will be hot water after the shower has been used for twenty minutes.

The inspector will check ceiling fans for the various speeds, if they are within reach, but not if the fans hang from a high ceiling.

The inspector will not normally check the furnace in the heat of the summer, nor will he check the AC and a swamp cooler in the dead of winter, so those items usually need to be discussed with the home's owners as to their performance.

It is nearly impossible to see the heat exchangers in the new furnaces and so the home inspector checks for a proper condensate drain from a condensing furnace, an electric shut off near the unit, a proper flue installation, the location and condition of the filter, and other things that can be seen.

The life expectancy of any item in the home is impossible to predict, and any home inspector that states an item has a certain number of years or months left is promising you the moon. However, it is possible for him to estimate the age of various components and to provide an average amount of time that such items last.

The roof is something that an inspector will visually inspect, and it is general practice to not walk on a tile roof, a wood shake roof, a metal roof, and an overly steep roof. These kinds of roofs are checked with high powered binoculars from the ground and with a ladder to the edge of the roof.

Likewise, the inspector generally does not walk through the attic as damage to the ceiling could occur. If ceiling stains are found or a suspect area of the roof is found, then it may be necessary for the inspector to try to reach that area in the attic with the understanding by the homeowner that even with extreme care some sheetrock joints could crack.

After I had been a home inspector for over five years and with well over 1700 inspections under my belt, I came up with a list of the top ten most common findings. Here they are, in no particular order:

First, the door from the garage to the house is not self-closing or the closer does not work properly. This door should have a self-closing device that will close and latch the door on its own. The door opening should have a proper gasket around it. Also installing pet doors in this door is not allowed. The door is intended to be a fire barrier between the garage and the home so it needs to seal properly.

Second, dirty air filters for the AC/Heating system. An air filter is a relatively low cost item. A dirty air filter is a high cost item since it lowers the efficiency of the AC/Heating system and therefore costs more to operate it. Experts recommend changing filters every 30 days in order to add life to the AC/Furnace unit and to help eliminate dust and odors in the home.

Third, water softener drain hose without an air gap device. A water softener drain hose shoved down inside of a drain pipe under certain unusual conditions may be able to act like a straw and suck back sewer water into the drinking water of the home. An air gap device is just a few dollars and very easy to install and will prevent a cross connection.

Fourth, rain gutter downspouts that discharge water next to the foundation. Downspouts during a hard rain storm can discharge as much as four gallons a minute. This is a lot of water collecting by the foundation. The main cause of damage to a home is from water or

Downspout discharging near foundation.

moisture intrusion. Always direct the downspouts away from the home by at least six feet if possible.

Fifth, cracked or broken concrete roofing tiles. It is extremely difficult to determine why roofing tiles crack. I do know that if a home is along a golf course fairway there is a good chance a golf ball may hit the roof and break a roofing tile. Every couple of years it may be a good idea to have a roofer take a look at the roof and replace any tiles that have cracked or slid out of place. A well-maintained roof protects the home better from moisture or other damage from the elements.

Broken roof tile.

Sixth, ground fault circuit interrupters (GFCI) not working. A GFCI is an electrical receptacle with two small buttons on it, one labeled test and the other labeled reset. This GFCI is designed to keep a person from being electrocuted. Normally the unit will last approximately eight to ten years. They are not costly to replace and are a very important safety device in a home. Test it monthly by plugging in a night light, for example, and then depressing the test button. The light should go out. Reset the unit and the light should come back on. If the GFCI does not work like this then it may be defective, and you should call a qualified electrician.

Seventh, loose fittings on sink drain pipes and traps. Most of the time the drain pipe and trap under a sink are made of plastic. The connections or fittings between parts are plastic as well and they tend to work loose. Check these fittings a couple of times a year, and if loose, tighten by hand. Do not use any kind of wrench or pliers.

Eighth, exterior doors with bad weather stripping. A 1/8 inch gap under an exterior door is equivalent to a two inch hole in an exterior wall. A lot of air and dust can enter the home through such an opening. Keeping the weather stripping and threshold gasket in good shape will save homeowners many dollars in the long run.

Ninth, lights that won't come on. As a home inspector I do not change bulbs. If a light does not come on it may or may not be just a burned out bulb, but I need to make mention of it in my report. Outside lights are sometimes on a dusk to dawn sensor and won't come on until dark. I will make mention of this as well.

And lastly, water heater relief valve discharge tubes missing, undersized, or improperly installed. If the temperature and pressure (T&P) relief valve on a water heater should open due to a problem with the water heater, the discharging water or steam could be scalding hot. The discharge tube cannot be a rubber hose. It has to be a solid material such as copper tubing of a proper size, usually ¾ inch. This tube must go to within six inches from the floor so the escaping hot water or steam will be directed to the floor and allow a person to access the water heater and shut it down. If this discharge tube drips or leaks, it normally means the relief valve needs to be replaced. An experienced plumber can do the job for you. Never, ever, plug up the end of this tube or remove the tube and plug the end of the relief valve. A blocked T&P value or discharge tube is an explosion waiting to happen.

Water Heater T&P valve with copper discharge tube extending to within 6" of the floor for safety.

While adding these ten items to a regular maintenance routine will ensure a safer and more energy efficient home, it's only a place to start. Remember, when problems arise, consult a professional. The money saved by doing it yourself is not worth the price you may pay if your family's safety or your home's integrity is compromised. You don't know what you don't know.

CHAPTER 4: WHAT DOES AN INSPECTOR DO?

In addition to my top ten findings, I have seen some crazy things in the dozen or so years I've spent inspecting homes. The first thing that comes to mind is a crawlspace I inspected several years ago. The floor above had evidently begun to sag in places, and someone had nailed 2x4s to brace the floor joists by standing the 2x4 up on a brick then nailing the other end to the joist. The crawlspace looked like a forest! I had to make my way through and around the 2x4's to complete my inspection.

In another home, an old one, the breaker panel was the kind with cartridge fuses in it. I suppose the fuses kept blowing because someone replaced them with lengths of copper tubing cut to the size of a cartridge fuse! I wrote this one up as a major safety concern and recommended that a licensed electrician correct this hazard ASAP! Then in

Mastic repair. Mastic is intended only as a temporary fix.

an attic of yet another old home, I saw three discarded furnaces! I guess it was too much trouble to remove them.

Not long ago, in a new home that had never been lived in, I found the furnace installation manual on top of the furnace burners. If that furnace had been started up with that manual on the burners, there would have been a fire for sure!

In another brand new home, also never having been lived in, I was puzzled looking at the windows in the living room, something just did not look right. On closer examination, I saw that one window was in backwards making it impossible to open that window from the inside.

It never ceases to amaze me how far a home owner will go to fix it himself. For example, I saw an oil burning furnace draft damper sealed shut by the home owner making the furnace into a time bomb without a timer. Another home had an oil burning furnace with a string and metal chisel hanging from the damper to keep the damper shut.

Up on a roof of another home around the vent pipes and the chimney there must have been seven layers of mastic to help seal water leaks. Mastic, in case you are not familiar with it, is normally a tar-like material that is applied with a spatula or trowel or putty knife. Even though this product is found in hardware stores, mastic is not approved for anything more than an emergency type of repair. Proper flashing is always recommended to stop water leaks around vent pipes and chimneys.

One home I inspected had a two gallon bucket under the kitchen sink full of water and drips of water coming from the trap fitting. As I was looking at this the owner saw my concern and casually said, "Oh

CHAPTER 4: WHAT DOES AN INSPECTOR DO?

I was about to fix that." How long do you think it takes to fill a two gallon bucket one drip at a time? That homeowner must have had his good intentions for quite a while.

Pulling back the shower curtain of another home revealed the most disgusting tub I have ever seen. Amazingly, it was still being used by the family!

One home about 50 years old revealed that the owners evidently got tired of the shower since they had installed a bathtub, but left the shower intact. However they must have needed some additional storage room so they added shelving in the shower to make it a linen closet.

On a funny side I was inspecting a vacant home with the buyer present. He looked on as I looked into the attic hatch in the garage. "Is there anything in there?" he asked. I proceeded to list the contents, "Two Christmas tree stands, four car tires, three bicycles, nine Halloween yard figurines, two football helmets, one mannequin, three rolls of carpet…" At that point he stopped me and asked me if I was joking around. "Nope," I said, "come up here and look for yourself." So he stuck his head in the attic opening. I won't write what he said, but his comments were something along the lines of "How in the world did someone get all of this stuff up here and how in the world am I going to get this stuff out of here without killing myself?" You can fill in the colorful wording on your own.

I guess when a home inspector has been in this business a while he should not be surprised at what he runs across.

I was inspecting a home that had been repossessed and the owners had moved all their things out. As I walked into the living room/

dining room area I noticed that the walls were painted two different colors. I could easily see where the entertainment center, the sofa, loveseat, china hutch and book shelf had been positioned. Someone had not bothered to move them, but simply painted around these items!

Mice in the furnace

In a kitchen one time as I was looking under the sink I suspected I had found someone's stash from an automotive store. The drains were all composed of radiator hoses and duct tape!

Dogs are not any fun to run into. I pulled up at the curb in front of one home and while I was getting my gear together I could hear behind me a barking dog that sounded like it was getting closer fast. Turning around I faced a very upset and mean-looking dog coming at me as if to tear my leg off. A woman in a robe was gently and casually calling for the dog in a sweet voice. Meanwhile I was looking for a weapon of some kind to use for self-defense. The dog approached to arm's length still looking like a graduate from a police K-9 training facility. All the while this woman strolled towards the dog calling in her sweet, tender voice for it to come to her. After counting the dog's teeth and seeing they were all sparkling white, I decided to get back into the truck. The woman ended up putting a leash on the dog and taking it to the backyard. Later she remarked to me not to mind "Fido" as he "just has to get used to strangers." I wondered if Fido had to get "used to strangers" the same way someone would get used to eating spicy food - one tiny bite at a time.

One home I inspected had a concrete tile roof with the heating/cooling unit mounted on the roof. In the area of the unit, the roofing was asphalt shingles, which is common. From the ground, I could see some patching had been performed. So I got onto the shingled portion of the roofing to carefully inspect the silicon seal and tar repairs. In the blink of an eye my left leg went through the roof all the way up to my hip. I would have liked to have had a video camera recording this as I never felt myself going through the roof and then getting back up on my feet. It happened so fast it was like a rattle snake strike, just a blur. When I was on my feet again I felt a minor pain in my small finger on my left hand, and found that it was bleeding from a small cut. My left hip hurt as well, and the next day a huge, black bruise appeared.

The resulting hole in the roof was about the size of a watermelon and I told the home owner, an elderly woman, what had happened. The home was in a PUD so she said she would call the Home Owner's Association president. I told her I had taken photos from the outside and needed to go up into the attic to see this area from the attic side. Once in the attic I could see, to my horror that a huge area of the roofing had been leaking for a long time. I determined that I was just lucky that only one of my legs went through the roof. With the hole thoroughly photographed, I returned to the kitchen where I printed the photos and presented them to the HOA president. I explained what had happened and upon seeing the photos he said something to the effect of "That #@!#$%%@# handyman! I will have a roofer come out right now and get this roof fixed and then go have a talk with that %#$@$@@# handyman!"

Another day as I was inspecting a quadplex, I began to remove the breaker panel to check the wiring and connections inside the panel, when sparks shot out of the panel around the screw I was taking out. I immediately stopped, located the manager and informed him of the sparks. He replied, "Oh, I can fix that." Then he proceeded to remove the panel, while I watched from 10 feet away - amazed at his daring deed. He removed the panel, found that the screw had nicked a wire inside the panel (the screw was an improper type for an electric panel) and then to my wonderment he got some electric tape and wrapped it around the nick, all without killing the power to the panel! Turning to me he said, "There. Now it is ok." Not in my book! I wrote it up in my report recommending a trained electrician inspect this panel.

At about 8:00 am one day, a realtor and I arrived at an occupied home at which the owner was reported to be out of town. I inquired of the realtor regarding the vehicle in the driveway, asking if the owner was indeed home. The realtor confirmed that the owner was gone, but to be safe, we knocked and rang the doorbell before entering and since the home was quite large we hollered to anyone in the home, "We are here to do a home inspection." There was no response so we proceeded to walk around inside the home getting an idea of how the home was laid out while keeping an eye out for occupants. Seeing no one, the realtor left and I set up my laptop and printer in the kitchen. About 20 minutes later as I walked down a hallway, out of a room came a man wearing a t-shirt and holding his under shorts in his hand, looking like he had just woken up, and asking if I was the inspector. "Yes, I am," I replied. I asked him where he was while we checked the home and hollered. He stood there with nothing on but the shirt and his under shorts still in his hand and said that he had been in the den sleeping on the couch. It was just my luck that the den was the one room we did not check for a sleeping person.

Well, that brings to mind another story. Ringing the door bell, I waited on the doorstep when a younger woman with wet hair and a small towel wrapped around her opened the door asking, "Are you the inspector?" "Uh, yes and if you don't mind I will begin with the outside of the house and the roof." I told her I will be coming inside in 45 minutes or so, hopefully giving her time to get some clothes on first.

Doing home inspections is what I love to do most, next to spending time with my family. Each home is a new experience. Each one tells a story, and the people I meet are mostly wonderful. And those who aren't are rare. For the most part, the people I meet make my day.

Chapter 5: Types of Inspections

Typically my clients are homebuyers. It's common nowadays for homebuyers to request an inspection on a home they are purchasing. Homeowners, even those not involved in the sale of a home, can also benefit from periodic inspections. The following list describes a few different types of inspections available. Any one of them or a combination may be just what a homeowner needs.

Warranty Inspections

Applicable only for new homes. The purpose is to identify deficiencies before the one or two year warranty expires. For homeowners of newly built homes, the thought of getting a brand new home inspected for potential defects might seem an unnecessary expense, but experts say problems can be present in even the newest homes.

It is fairly common for builders to offer a new construction one-year warranty which covers many aspects of repair and replacement throughout the house. Take advantage of the opportunity to document construction defects before your 12-month builder's warranty expires.

An independent home inspector can provide a thorough and detailed inspection report, often on-site.

As newly built homes age over a year's time, it is typical for various items to change. Structural, mechanical or cosmetic issues commonly develop within a recently built home. The homeowner's best bet is to catch the problem early.

With homes less than a year old, I rarely find situations that are a major cause for concern. However, I do often find conditions that could lead to major problems. For example, a recent inspection revealed a broken roof ridge tile. This tile needs to be replaced so that moisture will be prevented from penetrating the home through the roof. In another home I observed water puddling on the basement floor from a leaky bathtub above. Obviously this is a situation that should not be allowed to continue. Something else I see quite often is loose plumbing fixtures such as faucets or p-traps or toilets. These loose fixtures are all sources of potential leaks.

Another reason to have a new construction warranty inspection is to receive helpful home maintenance and cost-saving techniques regarding various systems throughout the home. Think of the report as a homeowner's operations manual. Learning how to properly maintain and operate your home's systems can help minimize future problems or costly repairs.

Pre-listing Inspections

An examination paid for by the seller before the home is put on the market. This report gives a homeowner an opportunity to take care of things that could be wrong before they are found by a potential buyer's inspector. With a pre-listing inspection report a seller is prepared for the negotiation process with prospective buyers.

Believe me, as a home seller you don't want it brought to your attention at the last minute that the furnace requires replacement or that the water heater leaks. When faced with that sort of unpleasant surprise, there are only a couple of possibilities, and both are bad for sellers. The buyers will either want to negotiate a lower purchase price to cover the cost of the repairs, or they will want to void the contract and find another home.

When you as the seller are able to show a recent inspection report to prospective buyers, it lends support to your statements that the home is in good shape. The report and any repair receipts provide buyers with proof of a home's condition inside and out, creating an environment of trust and goodwill between sellers and buyers. This can reduce stress amongst all parties and eliminate the chances of unknown problems that can cause sales to fall through.

A pre-listing inspection can help the owner, with advice from their agent, decide which, if any, projects to address before listing the home, correcting problems and eliminating last-minute repair hassles that could delay closing. For any projects not undertaken, the owner can obtain cost estimates for needed work. Sellers then have information which allows them to offer an adjustment to the listing price if needed.

Annual Home Maintenance Inspections

Deferred maintenance items can add up to big repair costs if left unattended for too long. Every home needs an annual inspection, conducted by the homeowner or a professional, to find problems early and minimize repair costs.

Each year, many homeowners successfully complete home repair and improvement projects. The reasons vary. It could be that some just can't afford to hire a contractor or it could be that some enjoy the challenge or diversion of working with their hands. Whatever the reason, home repairs and remodeling can be a great source of satisfaction and pleasure.

Some homeowners, at times don't seem to be able to judge when a task is beyond their skills. Painting, wallpapering and simple carpentry usually don't cause much problem. It's the more complex work such as electrical, plumbing, heating and structural where problems arise.

Corrugated pipe under a sink. The corrugation can trap solids allowing them to build up and cause a clog.

With every report I include a checklist of maintenance items for the client to guide them when inspecting the home for areas needing attention.

Home Energy Audit

This inspection is geared toward homeowners who want to save energy. Designed to help identify the best ways to save energy, homeowners can do it themselves with an online guide or contact their energy provider.

Termite Inspections

Termite infestation probability varies from state to state, however termites are found in every state. Where I live, in Southwest Utah, the probability is moderate to heavy according to the 2000 edition of the International Residential Code. Where termites are an issue, termite inspections should be performed regularly. A termite inspection is a visual inspection of the readily accessible areas of a home for evidence of wood-destroying insects (WDI) and wood-destroying organisms (WDO). The inspector will visually inspect the entire interior of a home (including accessing and entering any sub-space such as basements and crawlspaces) and exterior of the property.

Roof Inspections

The National Roofing Contractors Association (NRCA) recommends two roof inspections each year - once in the fall and once in the late spring - before and after the tough winter season, especially in colder climates. A roof could be leaking two to four years before evidence shows up on the interior of the home. By then, dry rot, fungus, insulation damage or other major problems may exist.

Pool & Spa Inspections

This type of report will address safety concerns and maintenance items. Have it done annually or whenever you suspect a problem.

Sewer Inspections

A visual inspection of the inside of the sewer pipe using a specially designed video camera mounted on the end of a sewer "snake." This is ideal for finding obstructions such as tree roots or destructive leaks.

Septic System Inspections

To be conducted at least every three years, according to the EPA. The inspection should include locating the system, uncovering access holes, flushing the toilets, checking for signs of back up, measuring the scum and sludge layers, identifying any leaks, inspecting mechanical components and pumping the tank if necessary.

Air Duct Inspections

Similar to a sewer inspection, air ducts can be inspected using a video camera. This would likely be done before and after air duct cleaning which is done to improve indoor air quality. The frequency of cleaning and inspecting air ducts is a matter of personal choice for homeowners.

Mold Testing

Mold is found in every home. There are over one hundred million different types that have been identified. Testing will reveal which types are present in your home and whether or not they are of a type dangerous to a person's health. Schedule an inspection when buying or if you suspect a problem.

Possible mold.

Water Quality Testing

Water quality testing applies to homeowners who have private wells. Here in Utah, the Utah State University Extension office suggests testing every year. The Utah Department of Environmental Quality and local health departments have no regulatory authority over private wells (your state may be different). Therefore, private well owners have to assume the responsibility of not only testing their water but also maintaining their private wells. Help for homeowners can be found at *http://extension.usu.edu/waterquality/htm/homeownerswater.*

Special Inspections

At times homeowners need a second opinion on a specific problem or concern. Home inspectors are one source to which homeowners can turn.

Radon Testing and Indoor Air Quality

The Utah Department of Environmental Quality recommends testing for radon in conjunction with real estate transfers or every three to five years. Read more about radon at *www.radon.utah.gov*. Also, a "Citizen's Guide to Radon" is available from the EPA website.

Lead-based Paint Testing

Generally applies to homes built prior to 1978. The EPA offers a helpful booklet, "Protect Your Family From Lead in Your Home" on their website.

Home inspectors provide many services in addition to a home buyer's inspection. The various inspections listed in this chapter may be provided by a home inspector or they may be available from another source. In any case, it doesn't hurt to ask. If your home inspector can't provide the service, he may know someone who can.

Part 2: Down & Dirty

Chapter 6: Components of an Average Home

As mentioned before, an average size home of about 2500 square feet will have over 3000 component parts. It's a complex series of systems working in tandem to create a comfortable living environment. As it would be near to impossible to address every home's situation due to the variations that exist, only a representative sampling of a home's major systems will be discussed here: electrical, plumbing, heating and cooling, structure, and building envelope.

Section 6.1: Electrical

Your home's electrical systems may seem bewildering with all the wires hidden inside the walls, switches, outlets, and fixtures and appliances. What seems complex at first can be understood with a simplified explanation.

Electric service begins at the local electricity distributor. From the supplier, electricity enters a home, either underground or overhead, through a conduit and a meter. The wires then enter the service panel

CHAPTER 6: COMPONENTS OF AN AVERAGE HOME

to connect to their respective buss bars inside - usually two hot, one neutral, and one ground buss. Circuit breakers cover the hot buss bars. Their role is to act as a safeguard against short circuits and overloads by tripping when a dangerous condition arises. Homeowners should know how to reset a breaker. Often it must be flipped to the "off" position before being turned back on. Additionally, power can be turned off or on as desired using the breaker as a switch.

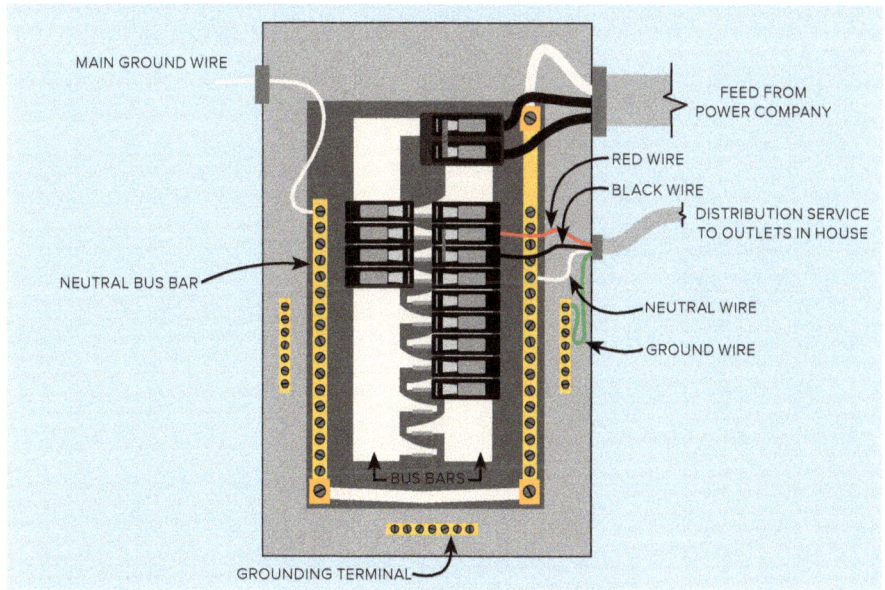

Main electrical panel with cover removed for inspection.

Older homes may have a fuse panel. Fuses will be either a round screw-in type or the larger cartridge type mounted in a fuse block that can be pulled from the main panel. For greatest safety, blown fuses must be replaced with the correct amperage rating. Although a larger amperage fuse may fit the socket, it will not protect the circuit properly. In one home I inspected with the cartridge type fuses, the homeowner had replaced a blown fuse with a length of copper tubing.

The electrical system may function like that, but without the protection from the fuse, it is also a fire hazard.

Electricity is distributed throughout the home by "hot" wires leaving the main panel to deliver power to a device (like a light fixture or appliance). These hot wires normally have black insulation. If a cable is the type with two hot leads it will also have a red insulated wire. It is the nature of electricity to seek to complete a circuit. A circuit is complete when the electricity has traveled from the device back to the panel. The path back to the panel uses the "neutral" wire, which is most often insulated with white.

Sometimes a break occurs in the planned path for the electricity. This is called a short. Sometimes overloads happen when too many appliances are plugged into one circuit. In these situations, the ground wire, which is usually green (or bare copper), offers the electrical current an alternate path to the panel. Once at the service panel, the ground diverts electricity to a safe destination which may be a long metal rod buried outside the house (the grounding rod) or the home's water pipes.

Cable, the name electricians have for electrical wires, comes covered by a flexible plastic sheathing. Technically, the correct name is non-metallic-sheathed (NM) cable, but it is often referred to by the brand name "Romex" the same way facial tissues are often called "Kleenex" or a photocopier is known as a "Xerox" machine. There are different types of cable for different uses. The differences are in the gauge (thickness) and in the number of leads inside. For example, NM 14-2G means that the cable is nonmetallic, each conducting wire is 14 gauge, there are two conducting wires inside (1 neutral, 1 hot), and a ground wire.

CHAPTER 6: COMPONENTS OF AN AVERAGE HOME

Properly installed electrical systems are very safe and efficient. Some basic knowledge on the part of homeowners can help prevent safety problems, though. Homeowners should know where the main electrical disconnect is located and how and when to use it. It is helpful to have the breakers or fuses clearly labeled in the main panel. Identify which breakers or fuses control which groups of outlets and switches. Also, know which outlets are GFCI protected.

According to OSHA 1910.399, a GFCI, is defined as "...a device whose function is to interrupt the electric circuit to load when a fault current to ground exceeds some predetermined value, that is less than that required to operate the over current protective device of the supply circuit."

Or to put it another way, GFCIs are designed to shut off electric power within as little as 1/40 of a second. It works by comparing the amount of current going into the electric equipment to the amount of current returning from the equipment along the circuit conductors. If the difference is more than about five milliamperes, the GFCI interrupts the current to prevent electrocution. Or to put it yet another way, GFCIs save lives.

GFCI protection should be found anyplace that there is, or could be, a wet or moist environment such as around the bathroom sinks, kitchen sinks, in a garage, crawlspace, basement, around a swimming pool, hot tub or spa, a jet tub in the bathroom, a water feature, or laundry sink to name a few. A single GFCI can protect several receptacles so you may find one unit protecting more than one bathroom.

To ensure proper operation, a GFCI receptacle should be checked each month, and after a severe thunder and lightning storm. A simple way for a home owner to test them is by plugging a night light into the receptacle and pressing the test button. The light should go out and stay out until the reset button is pressed. The GFCI is defective if the light does not go out and stay out until the reset button is pressed, or if the test button cannot be depressed, for example because it's been painted over, or if the reset button will not reset the GFCI. Homeowners should not rely on a GFCI that fails this test. A qualified electrician should inspect, possibly rewire, and, if necessary, replace the unit. Proper installation of GFCIs requires significant knowledge of electrical wiring and should only be performed by a qualified electrician.

As a side note, it is not a good idea to plug a freezer or refrigerator into a GFCI protected receptacle, such as the second fridge in the garage. It is common for the GFCI to trip due to the start up surge when the compressor comes on interrupting the power to the item. If the freezer or refrigerator is in the garage it is possible that this could go undetected for some time until some unknowing person opens the door on the unit and finds it full of spoiled food.

If you live in an older home where no GFCIs are installed do not be deceived that just because you or a loved one have not been injured that it will not happen. Electric shocks are responsible for about 1000 deaths in the United States each year, or about 1% of all accidental deaths. Believe it or not, in a 1950's home I inspected once, I found one receptacle in the kitchen hanging out of the wall next to the sink with a computer type surge protector strip plugged into it. And into that surge strip the occupants had plugged the toaster, coffee maker, and an extension cord. The extension cord ran across the counter top to power the washing machine! It was about the most unsafe situation you could imagine. It could have been corrected, and the occupants of the home made safer, by repairing the electrical outlets and upgrading at least one of them to GFCI. The expense to upgrade existing outlets to GFCI protection is minimal compared to the cost of someone getting hurt.

The GFCI, as a safety device, should not come second to common sense and cautious behavior whenever using electrical appliances. Wherever there is a situation where water and electricity may come into contact, people need to be extra careful and follow any recommended safety precautions.

AFCIs circuit breakers are becoming as common as ground fault circuit interrupter receptacles(GFCIs). The term AFCI stands for arc fault circuit interrupter. Unlike a GFCI, the AFCI circuit breaker's purpose is to protect against fires caused by unwanted arcing in the home electrical system. Arcing faults are one of the major causes of home fires. According to the Consumer Product Safety Commission, over 40,000 fires annually are attributed to home electrical wiring. These fires result in over 350 deaths and over 1,400 injuries each year.

Arcing is the flow of electricity through the air from one conductor to another. It can occur when a plug is pulled from a socket or when a switch is opened. This is normal and generally not a problem. The problem arises with arcing faults which often occur in damaged or deteriorated wires and cords. Increased heat generated by an arc can ignite nearby combustible materials such as wood, paper, or carpet. Some causes of damaged and deteriorated wiring include:

- accidental piercing of a wire's insulation from sharp metal objects puncturing the wall surface, such as nails used to hang pictures or staples used to secure cables,

- outlets or switches which may have been improperly installed,
- electrical cords from appliances such as lamps which become caught in doors or under furniture,
- plugs in an outlet compromised by furniture being pushed tightly against them,
- natural deterioration from growing older, and
- exposure of electrical cords to heat from air vents and sunlight.

While conventional circuit breakers are designed to respond to overloads and short circuits, AFCIs use specially designed sensing circuitry to continuously monitor the flow of the electrical current. When conditions indicate that arcing is possible the AFCI breaker trips and stops the flow of electricity. As a result, the potential for a fire to occur is consequently reduced.

It is important to note that although AFCIs have been found to be successful in preventing home fires from arcing faults, they cannot eliminate them completely. In some cases, it is possible for the arc to cause a fire before the AFCI detects the situation and interrupts the circuit. It is also possible for some appliances to cause the AFCI to trip when no danger of arcing is present.

AFCI circuit breakers have a test button and look similar to GFCI circuit breakers. AFCI receptacles also have a test button similar to a GFCI receptacle. As with GFCIs, AFCIs should be tested monthly to ensure that they are working properly and providing the protection for which they were designed.

One electrical defect sometimes found in homes during an inspection is improper wiring of receptacles, also known as outlets.

Improperly wired outlets are a potential shock hazard and can cause electrical equipment to work harder. Many of today's electronic devices such as TVs, stereos, DVD players, and computers are intended for use with a 3-prong receptacle which has the power flowing from one direction of the outlet. An outlet that is reverse-wired may result in the device having a shorter life span.

The correct way for all receptacles to be wired is that the hot or live (black) lead is connected to a specific side of the outlet, and the neutral (white) lead to the other. When an appliance is plugged into an outlet and turned on the electrical circuit is completed allowing power to flow. The circuit is supposed to open and close on the hot side – so that when the appliance is switched off, there will be no voltage inside the device or receptacle. You may have noticed that the openings on an outlet are not identical. On the typical receptacle, the hot side is the shorter of the two openings, whereas the neutral is the longer of the two. The prongs on the appliance's plug will correspond by having one of the prongs wider so the hot and the neutral sides line up correctly.

The condition where the hot (black) and neutral (white) wire connections are connected to the wrong sides of the outlet is known as reverse polarity. Modern receptacles have screws of different colors to assist installers with making the connection correctly. The hot wire must be connected to the brass screw, while the neutral wire should be connected to the silver screw and the copper ground wire connects to the green screw.

Sometimes the hot and ground wires are incorrectly placed. This is a very dangerous situation. The outlet box itself as well as housing of the appliance plugged into the receptacle, perhaps the base of a lamp or the metal cover of a toaster, may be energized. In this case, should you come in close contact; your body will complete the circuit to ground and you will feel a shock!

Allow me to share another example of an unsafe condition. About 2:00 am one morning when our boys were very young a loud noise woke up both my wife and I. I got up to investigate and found the ceiling fan in our boys' room had fallen to the floor. I disconnected the wiring and examined the fan's mounting plate. I discovered that a screw holding the metal plate to the ceiling had snapped in half. Once the stores opened up in town I purchased a fan and installed the new one.

Unbelievably, this happened again a short time later, not in our home but in a vacant home I was inspecting. The realtor was there to unlock the door. While my laptop was booting up I started all of the ceiling fans so they would be running at proper speed during my inspection then I returned to the laptop to proceed with the inspection.

Just a couple of minutes later we heard a CRASH! And both the realtor and I dashed to the rear of the house where the noise had come from to find a ceiling fan laying on the bedroom floor. Since I had seen this same thing happen in my own home I examined the fan and the mounting hardware, only to find this time that someone had used sheetrock screws to mount the bracket to the ceiling, probably installed by an inexperienced do-it-yourselfer.

I further found that this home owner also had simply taped the wiring splices together instead of using wire nuts. A quick check of the other three fans in the home showed them to be of the same design, and even though they seemed to be working properly, I shut them all off immediately. I included a comment in the report about the ceiling fan falling to the floor and what I found, suggesting that it may be wise to have an electrician check the other fans to see if they had been installed in the same unsafe manner.

Each of these various electrical defects can be tested for and corrected. Although some homeowners may feel confident performing this work themselves, in most cases, electrical work is best left to a qualified professional electrician.

Section 6.2: Plumbing

Another of a home's systems is the plumbing. We are fortunate to live in a day and age when we have running water and indoor toilets. Water enters the home through the supply lines then branches to various locations in the home through the distribution piping. After use, the water enters the waste water piping which leads to the sewer system. The water supply and waste system will be either publicly provided or private. Either way, plumbing components are included as a usual part of a home inspection.

"Toilet is loose to the floor. Contact a qualified professional to tighten." If the toilet is really loose to the floor I add the comment "Recommend asking a plumber to evaluate the seal, flange, and toilet, and look for any floor damage and advise on the cause and cure." This comment appears in my reports now and then. Loose toilets are a fairly common finding in home inspections and can be an indicator of more serious problems.

A basic understanding of toilet installation is necessary in order to understand the implications of a loose toilet. A toilet is attached to a toilet floor flange (made of cast iron or plastic) which, in turn, is attached to the sewer drain pipe. The toilet and the flange are connected together with "closet bolts" which are also referred to as "Johnny bolts" or "hold-down bolts." The bolts were probably covered at one time, but more often than not the covers are missing and the bolts are visible at the base of the toilet.

Within the space between the toilet and the flange is a wax ring. The wax ring seals the connection between the toilet and the sewer pipe. The ring keeps sewer gases from entering the house and prevents leaks at the base of the toilet. But over time, the toilet can become loose, causing the seal at the wax ring to break allowing potential gas and/or water leaks. It is possible for continuous movement of the toilet to compress a portion of the ring so it no longer seals the connection between the toilet and the flange. Once this happens, the ring must be replaced.

A toilet can be loose for a number of reasons. It may be loose closet bolts, a hidden leak which softens the floor material, a broken floor flange or a poor original installation, to name a few. If no signs of a leak are present and no unpleasant odors suggest a broken seal or flange, then the most probable cause is loose closet bolts which can simply be re-tightened.

A WORD OF WARNING

These bolts must be tightened carefully and evenly, a little at a time on each side. This tightening operation is a "feel" thing gained from experience. It is *very easy* to be overly aggressive and

actually break the cast iron flange or even the porcelain toilet base. I recommend hiring an experience professional to tackle this project. It is cheaper to hire a professional than it is to replace a toilet!

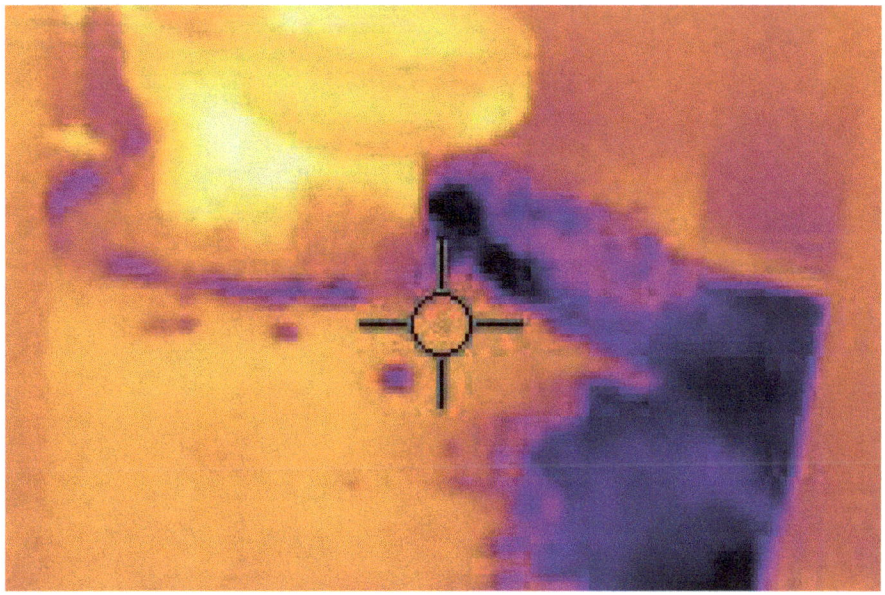

Infrared Image of moisture in bathroom floor. The damp areas appear purple or blue.

Toilets should be checked for movement every couple of years. When I inspect a home I test the toilets by standing over the bowl and placing a knee on each side of it and doing my version of "The Twist." If I can move the toilet with pressure from either knee, it is too loose. If loose fixtures are found, call a licensed plumber for further recommendation or repair. Consider replacing the wax seal when repairing loose toilets. It's a wise precaution against further, more serious issues.

A home inspection is not just about finding current problems, but also about uncovering possible future difficulties. Such it is when looking under sinks.

The pipes and P-traps under sinks in most homes today are plastic. I inspect these for leaks and check to see if they are tightly secured or not.

Several years ago when my son Wyatt was seven years old, he had a loose tooth that he would wiggle and tug on. One day it got loose enough that he easily pulled it out. I was thinking about this today as I inspected a home and found loose drain pipe fittings under a bathroom sink. Drain pipes are like teeth. If they are loose they may come apart, or out as with teeth.

My other son, Morgan, who was five, had no loose teeth at all, but a couple of days after Wyatt's tooth came out Morgan fell and hit his mouth pretty hard, knocking one of his top teeth out. Continuing the analogy, if drain pipe fittings are tight they are not a problem, but shoving trash cans, bleach bottles, cleaning gear, pots, pans, and such under sinks may knock a drain pipe apart or cause it to come loose so that it may begin to leak. I advise home buyers and sellers when I find an excessive amount of items packed under a sink that this condition may cause a problem at some time in the future. It may be best to unpack the area under the sink and store the items elsewhere.

Loose teeth and loose traps – neither one is desirable (unless you're 7 years old and looking forward to a visit from the tooth fairy). So make a point of checking under your sinks for loose drain pipe fittings. If any are found, forestall future leaks by tightening them. As always, seek help from a professional when in doubt about any repair.

While most distribution pipes are plastic, it's still possible to find galvanized piping in older homes. Galvanized piping is steel pipe coated with zinc to resist corrosion. It is dull silver or gray in color. Used for water distribution within the house, this type of pipe is likely to be found in homes built prior to 1950. It was used almost exclusively until that time. This plumbing product was used in an attempt to reduce or inhibit rusting. And that it does. However these pipes are not rust proof.

Rusted and leaking galvanized pipe.

Commonly, these pipes will rust from the inside out. As the pipe wears, rust and minerals accumulate and over time will restrict water flow. Both pressure and volume may be reduced by this corrosion. Eventually the pipe becomes blocked, or worse yet, bursts. A symptom of this condition is brownish water which initially flows through a fixture that may not have been used for a time. Another sign is fixtures that have become rust stained.

Leaky pipes are another potential problem. Galvanized pipes have threaded joints which may easily leak because the pipe is thinner at these connections. This type of pipe also fractures more easily than copper.

A third concern is electrolytic or galvanic action that will corrode the pipe when connected directly to copper. When used together the two dissimilar pipes should have a dielectric coupler (brass connector) between them to prevent damage.

Eventually these galvanized pipes, which have a life span of about 50 years, will need to be replaced. Since this limited lifespan has now expired, it is recommended that all galvanized plumbing in a home be replaced if the piping shows any signs of failure.

Water heaters, as part of the plumbing system in a home, are one item normally included in a home inspection. Their function is to provide hot running water within the home. In addition to the interior burn chamber, I include five readily visible items in my check: presence or absence of the discharge tube, proper ventilation, corroded fittings, rust on the shroud, and the presence or absence of a drip pan. A leak is a sign that the water heater is nearing the end of its lifespan and you will need to replace the unit soon.

Sometimes water heaters malfunction and the water in the tank may be heated to unsafe levels. Sometimes this super-heated water builds up pressure that needs to be released or the water heater will explode. For this reason water heaters are equipped with temperature and pressure (T&P) relief valves. This is a key safety feature of the water heater. This valve is either on the side of the water heater close to the top edge or it is on the very top of the water heater. This T&P relief valve has a very specific purpose. It is designed to release excessive pressure from the water heater in case of some kind of malfunction and to prevent the water heater from exploding. Many times I have seen this valve with a metal plug screwed into it or I have seen a metal plug screwed into where the valve used to be. Both cases will make the water heater into a bomb powerful enough to take out a wall in the house.

The safest condition is for the T&P relief valve to have a discharge tube of at least ¾ inch in diameter going from the valve to the outside of the house or to within a few inches of the floor, not to an unmonitored crawlspace. The purpose of the discharge tube is to direct the high temperature water and steam safely away in case the T&P valve opens. A person can then safely access the water heater to shut it off. If the discharge tube is too short or not installed, the discharging hot water or steam would be at face level and not allow a person to get near the water heater to shut it down. Should the discharge tube terminate in the crawlspace an opened or leaky valve could go unnoticed for quite some time. The discharged water would collect in the crawlspace causing other problems for the home.

The testing of the T&P valve lever is excluded from the home inspection. Although manufacturers recommended testing every three years, I would guess most homeowners don't bother with it. As such, if the lever is lifted for a test, a number of factors may cause it not to be able to be reset in its proper place – factors such as sediment in the water discharged, mild corrosion on the valve, damage to the metal of the lever, etc. When this occurs the entire valve must be replaced. In my inspection report, I inform homeowners or buyers that the valve needs periodic testing and then leave it up to them to see that it is done.

The following is a short list of seriously unsafe conditions I have seen at one time or another:

- T&P relief valve lever up against the wall so the T&P could never open.
- Missing discharge tube.
- Discharge tube too short in length - like 4 inches!
- Discharge tube made of garden hose.
- Discharge tube made of flex copper tubing.
- Discharge tube necked down to ¼ inch copper tubing.
- Discharge tube terminated in crawlspace (cannot easily see if it should be leaking or open. A lot of water can collect in the crawlspace before it might be discovered.)
- T&P missing and a metal plug in the hole.

T&P valve missing a discharge tube.

It's a simple matter to see that the T&P relief valve and discharge tube are properly and safely installed. In this case everyone's motto should be "Better safe than sorry."

At times a gas water heater is located in a closet inside the home. In this situation it is critical that the air inlet duct that brings in fresh air from the outside and the door louvers that vent air from the closet are never blocked. Proper combustion of the burner can only occur when the air is allowed to flow freely. Don't store items on top of the water heater, possibly blocking off the draft area for the flue. If any of these are blocked off with stored items there is a good chance that the water heater can produce deadly carbon monoxide gas.

Corrosion at the hot and cold water fittings on the top of the water heater is common. This mineral buildup is an indication of past seeping or dripping which may only have stopped because of the corrosion. The underlying cause of the problem is still present and although an active leak may not be visible today, the chance is good that a leak will occur one day in the future. In that instance a plumber may not be able to simply replace the leaky fittings without damaging the water heater due to the excessive corrosion.

On occasion rust will be found on the outer metal covering of the water heater. The presence of rust is not necessarily an indication of a leak. Frequently the source of the rust is a result of condensation caused by the combustion process. Water vapor is one of the predominant byproducts of gas combustion; therefore, a thorough check of the venting system is essential. Many gas-fired water heaters are returned as leaky when the real culprit was condensation fooling not only the inspector, but the plumber and property owner as well. In general condensation is greatest during winter and early spring when the water temperature entering the unit will be at its lowest. Seasonal differences in water temperature can vary by as much as 30°F.

It is important to note that excessive condensation can also cause the pilot light to go out due to water running down the flue tube onto the main burner. This situation will cause premature corrosion of the tank, but not necessarily the water heater's visible outer surface.

One more thing about a water heater, if it is inside the home and there is not a floor drain nearby, it is a good idea to have a drip pan installed under the heater to catch any drips or slight leaks that may occur, thus helping to prevent damage to the surface under the water heater.

Every now and then go look at your water heater. Look for signs of corrosion, rust, water leaks, drips, and moist areas around pipe fittings. Know how to shut off the water heater in case of an emergency. Know where your main water shut off valve is in case of a major water leak. Keep the water heater closet clear of all stored items, such as brooms, mops, plastic shopping bags, vacuum cleaners, etc. The unit has to be able to breathe properly in order to function properly. If you question whether your water heater is operating properly call a licensed plumber to evaluate it.

Since Southwest Utah is largely rural, I often have occasion to inspect homes with septic systems. Clients always have questions and I have found a few of them to be universal.

How does a septic system work? A septic tank is mainly a set of settling chambers. Waste water enters and stays for a while during which time the solids and scum separate from the liquid. The solids settle to the bottom and are then called sludge while the scum floats to the top. As more water enters the tank an equal amount is forced to leave and flow to the drain or leach field. So obviously, if a lot of water is flowing through the tank, there will not be enough time for solids to properly settle and the system will be unable to perform at its best. The system also becomes less efficient as the scum and sludge remaining in the tank increase.

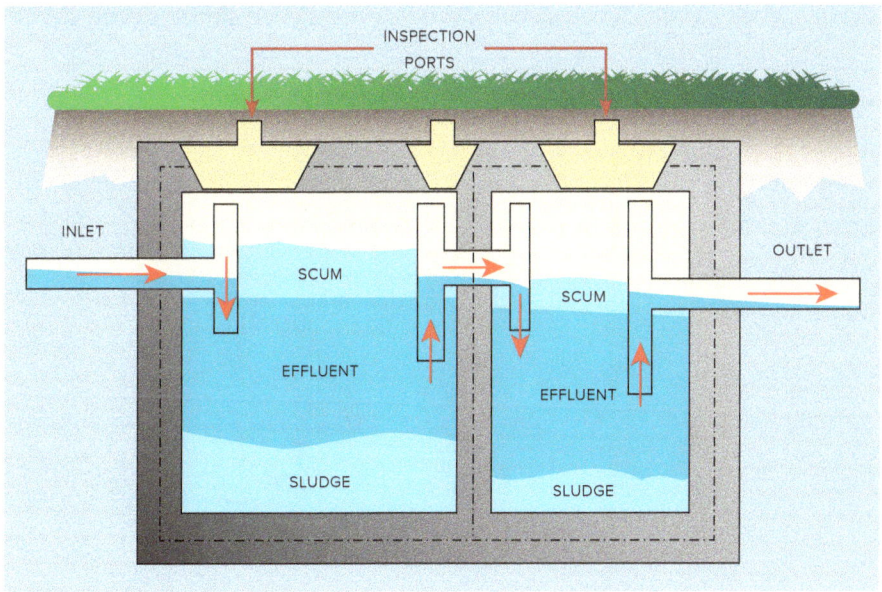

Multi-chamber septic tank.

Where is the septic tank? As a home inspector I can only report on visible items in and around the home. If I can find one of the covers I will note its location on a diagram in the report. Many times, however, the covers are hidden by dirt or debris and are not readily visible. Sometimes the location of the drain field is apparent and can give a clue as to the placement of the tank, but many times it's just not possible for me to determine the tank's position.

How often should I have the tank pumped? Of course, the answer depends on how heavily the system is used and the size of the tank. A family of two will not need a tank pumped as often as a family of seven with the same size tank. Most tanks need to be pumped every three to five years. As a general rule of thumb, septic tanks should be checked for buildup every one to three years until the pumping schedule becomes fairly predictable. Professionals will measure the amount of scum and sludge in the tank to determine whether it needs pumping. A more complete inspection includes determining the condition of the baffles and the pipe seals into and out of the tank.

In most cases septic system inspections are beyond the scope of a home inspection, although I know some inspectors in other states who do them. My inspection includes the plumbing system – checking for adequate water flow, slow drains, loose toilets and traps, etc. – but excludes the septic tank itself. When I am called to a home with a septic system I recommend that the clients contact a septic specialist to evaluate the system and provide information beyond what I included in the inspection report.

Section 6.3: Heating and Cooling

It would be difficult to name the types and combinations of heating and cooling systems I run across. This section will highlight a few systems and components.

Many of the homes I inspect have evaporative coolers or "swamp coolers" as they are sometimes called. This type of cooling system is ideal for a hot, dry climate like we have here in Southern Utah. Not only does it use seventy-five percent less electrical energy than a refrigerated central air-conditioning system, it works better as the outside temperature rises, operating best during the hottest part of the day.

How does an evaporative cooler work? Basically it uses a simple physical principle of evaporation. The evaporative cooler is essentially a sheet metal cube. The bottom of the cube is a pan about three inches high. This pan holds the water for the cooler. In this pan or reservoir is a water pump which discharges through a rubber tube to the top of the cube where it splits into four different tubes, each of these tubes going to one of the sides of the cube. Each side is a sheet metal panel with louvers in it designed to hold a pad made of aspen fibers, wood wool, plastic mesh or some other material. The tube wets the pads from the top. The water runs down the pad and drips back into the pan or reservoir. In the reservoir is a float valve that is connected to a small plastic tube, usually about ¼ inch in diameter that goes to a water source such as a water faucet to allow water to be added to the reservoir when necessary.

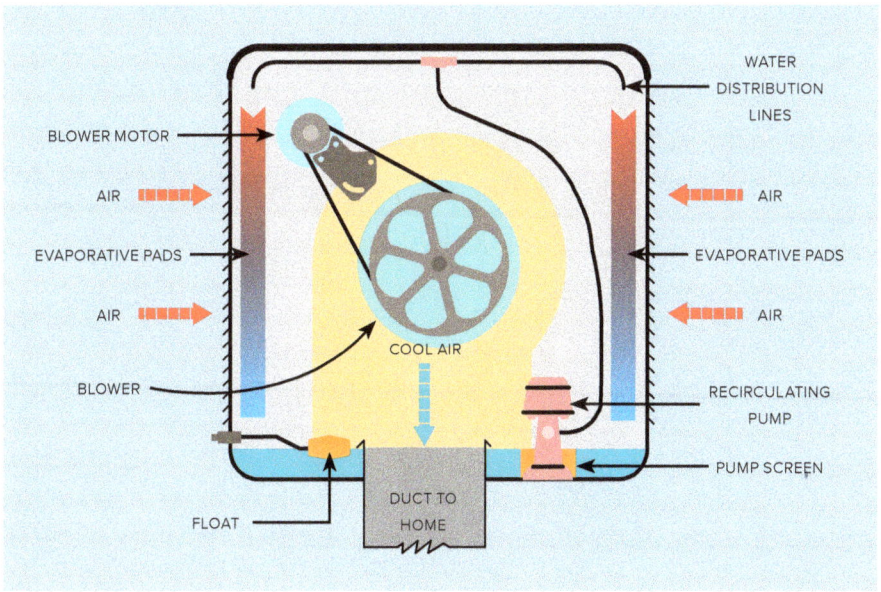

Swamp cooler.

Inside the cooler unit is a large motor and blower assembly that pulls air in through the pads, removing warmth from it as it passes over the pads. As such, air entering the home is usually 20-30 degrees cooler than the outside air. The blower then sends this cooled air into the home through a central register, usually in the hallway ceiling. This system is different from a central cooling system which has air registers in each room. There is also no thermostat on most systems and the unit is turned on and off as needed.

Since the evaporative cooling unit blows air into the home from outside, air flow is created as excess air is pushed out through open windows. The windows act in a similar capacity as a thermostat. The amount of cool air in any room of the house is regulated by the size of the window opening. A narrow gap traps warm air in the room while a wider opening allows more air out of the room and more fresh cool air to flow into the room.

The time limitations of a home inspection do not allow a home inspector to verify how well the unit works, just whether it is working or not and that the different components are in good shape or not. Things that I check on an evaporative cooler are:

- Are the cooling pads clean or heavy with mineral deposits?
- Does the blower operate on both high and low speeds?
- Does the water pump inside the cooler work to pump water out of the water reservoir pan to the pads?
- Does the float valve (inside the water reservoir pan that controls the level of the water) work as it should?
- Is the fan belt for the blower motor in good shape?

- And for roof-mounted units, is the overflow pipe on the reservoir connected to a hose or PVC pipe so any overflow water will not run down the roof over the shingles and cause premature wear of the shingles? I have seen countless times where the roofing shingles are in great shape except for the shingles between the evaporative cooler and the roof's edge. These shingles tend to be white in color and curled up from excessive water and or minerals constantly running over them.

Evaporative coolers need maintenance more often than central air conditioning systems. The specifics of what should be done will be depend on the system, but in general this includes a major cleaning and maintenance every season as well as routine inspection and cleaning throughout the season. With the power off to the cooler, drain and flush the water and remove scale and sediment from the water reservoir. Inspect and replace, or clean pads and filters. Inspect and clean the water distribution system. Cooler pads, fan belts, water pump, and float valve are items that may need replacing every couple of years or so. These items are not very expensive and are easy to install, thus making this system rather cost effective.

In the winter, it is a good idea to drain the reservoir and clean out any debris, and remove the pump so it does not freeze in the cold periods. A lot of people will choose to cover the evaporative cooler with a tarp so the winter winds do not find their way into the home. Sometimes the vent in the hallway ceiling will have a sheet of metal that can be slid across the vent to help stop cold air from entering the home.

Proper maintenance is necessary to receive optimum performance from your evaporative cooler. If the unit is on the roof or you feel the maintenance is beyond your abilities, then be sure to hire a professional to do the work for you.

In order to properly to maintain your home's systems, you need a little bit of knowledge. I am not only a home inspector, but also a resource for homeowners. For example one winter I had a man call me, wondering if he could ask me a question. "Sure thing!" I told him. He said that his furnace had been cycling on and off a lot. He could not figure it out. He called a heating repairman to come out and see what was wrong.

The repairman, after just a few minutes, presented an air filter that, in this man's words, "had a layer of dirt on it three inches thick." He said the heating repairman changed the filter, checked it for proper operation and was on his way.

The caller told me that now the furnace works great. His question to me was, "How much money does a dirty air filter waste and how often should the filter be changed?" I told the caller that I recommend changing the filter every 30 to 40 days, and from what I have learned in some of my continuing education courses, a clean filter can save up to $100 a year on your heating bill. I then told him that a clean filter also has been proven to add life to the furnace unit as the dirt a filter catches does not enter the furnace and cause premature wear inside the furnace.

It is a good idea to have your heating and cooling system serviced each year. Also I told the caller that a programmable thermostat, when programmed and set properly, will also save him money.

A thermostat is a device for controlling a home's heating and cooling systems so that the temperature in the home is maintained at or near a set temperature. The unit does this by sensing the room temperature, and when the room temperature varies from the setting on the thermostat, the heating or cooling system is activated. It is, fundamentally, a temperature sensitive switch.

While some thermostats control only a heating system, others have a switch that allows a homeowner to change the system from heating to cooling and to operate the fan separately. Some thermostats also allow the heating and cooling systems to be turned off.

With a dual control thermostat, once the unit is set to either HEAT or COOL, the thermostat temperature setting automatically controls the system by sensing the room temperature and activating the system as needed.

The FAN switch on the thermostat gives a homeowner the option of operating the fan without operating the heating or cooling system. Operating only the fan causes air to circulate throughout the home. AUTO is the setting normally used when the fan does not run continuously. In this setting the fan automatically cycles on and off as needed by the heating and cooling systems.

Typically a whole house heating or cooling system is either fully on or fully off. There is no way to vary the temperature from room to room (however, some homes do have more complicated systems capable of varying the heating or cooling of individual rooms, called "zones", but these are the exception). When the thermostat calls for heat, the furnace turns on at full capacity. When the thermostat senses that the desired temperature has been reached then the furnace turns off. Turning the thermostat higher will not heat a room, or the whole house, any faster. Similarly, turning the setting lower will not cause the air conditioning system to cool a room faster. It just causes the system to run longer to reach the set temperature.

Electronic or programmable thermostats automatically adjust the settings according to a schedule that the homeowner specifies. These can help save energy costs by allowing the temperature to be lower in winter or higher in summer when a home's occupants are away or sleeping.

Thermostats are very sensitive, and if they are not properly installed they won't operate as desired. Anticipator settings on the unit match its operation to the furnace. If set improperly the furnace may cycle off and on too frequently, or an incorrect alignment may allow the room temperature to drop too low or rise too high before the furnace comes on or goes off. In addition, the thermostat should be level, out of direct sunlight, and away from other heat sources.

When a problem arises with a thermostat and adjusting the settings correctly doesn't solve it, consider replacement rather than repair. If you need to change out a mechanical thermostat, think about upgrading it with a programmable electronic thermostat to enable your heating and cooling system to work more efficiently.

When mercury readings are dropping outdoors it's especially nice to be indoors in a warm environment. The heating and cooling systems are checked as a part of a home inspection. Homes with heat pumps generally prompt one main question: How do heat pumps work? The best way to answer this question is to start by explaining how an air-conditioner works.

An air conditioner has two parts – an evaporator inside the home and a condenser outside. Air is blown over the evaporator coil before it is distributed throughout the house by the duct work. The evaporator absorbs heat from the air passing over it and transfers it to the condenser outside. A fan blows on the condenser coil to dissipate the heat to the outdoors. You might think that an air conditioner cools your home's air, but actually it removes heat from the indoor air and transfers that heat to the outdoor air. When in cooling mode, a heat pump works exactly like an air-conditioner. It extracts heat from inside the home and transfers it to the outdoor air.

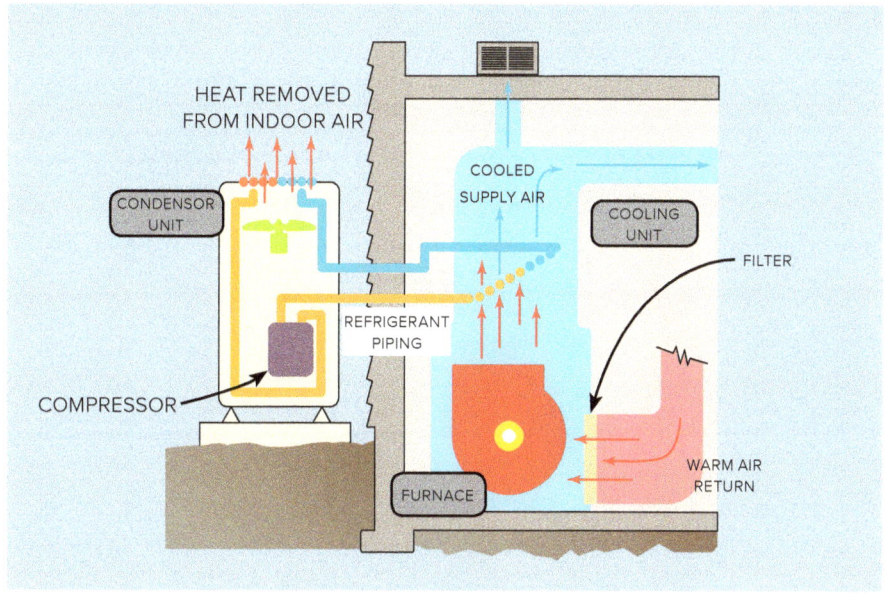

Central air conditioning and heating system.

Unlike an air conditioner, a heat pump has a reversing valve that reverses the process, so in the heating mode the unit collects heat from the outdoor air and transfers it inside to heat your home. Even when the air outside feels cold, it still contains some heat. Heat is extracted from the outside air by passing the air across the condensing coil in the outdoor unit. The heat is transferred indoors to the evaporator coil where it is released into the indoor air through the use of a fan.

In below freezing conditions, there may not be enough heat in the outside air to meet the demand of the thermostat setting, so an electric heater backup coil in the indoor unit helps to make up the difference to warm your house. Additionally, in very cold climates, the exterior unit should have a mechanism to defrost the coils periodically.

Central air conditioning and forced air furnaces are much more common in our area than heat pumps. As in most United States climates the outdoor-to-indoor temperature differential in Southwest Utah is greater in the winter than in the summer, and it is more difficult for the heat pump to move the heat. Hence the heat pump is less efficient in the winter. However, since a heat pump is only moving heat instead of making new heat, it is much more efficient than direct heating (like electric baseboard heaters), and easily able to transfer two to three times as much heat as can be directly generated with the same amount of electricity.

Other options for heating are wood burning stoves or fireplaces. Modern homes tend not to use wood burning fireplaces as the main source of heat. However, many home buyers still desire them for the sense of warmth and coziness they provide.

One of the most common problems with wood burning fireplaces, however, is that they smoke. In fact, a study by Environment Canada (the equivalent of the EPA) found that using a wood fire stove for only nine hours produces as much fine-particle pollution as a car does in a year.

The purpose of the chimney is to draw the smoke upward out of the home. Ideally, smoke should draw naturally up the chimney at all times. Sometimes a fireplace smokes while it's in use. If so, it may be that it's not designed properly or something is blocking the chimney and not allowing the smoke to exit.

A phenomenon labeled "cold hearth syndrome" describes two of the most common times for the fireplace to smoke. The fireplace and chimney are coolest when the fire has just been started and after it has burnt down. Once the chimney flue has had a chance to warm up, it will draw properly. However, in a "cold hearth" state, air will tend to flow down the chimney rather than up, a condition called back-draft. Remember, heated air rises while cool air falls. One tell-tale sign of chronic back-drafting is soot on the underside of the mantle.

Evidence of possible back-drafting.

Due to various reasons, some fireplaces will have more of a problem with back-drafting than others. One factor involved is chimney height. A taller chimney will draw better. Back-drafting may also occur when the fire is built too close to the front of the firebox or if the firebox is too shallow.

If a problem is indicated, here are some steps homeowners can take. First, call a local certified chimney sweep and schedule an inspection and cleaning. Second, make sure the fire grate is back as far as it will go before building a fire. Third, check to make sure the damper is open when the fireplace is in use. Next, install glass doors or a fire screen. Reducing the effective opening size of the fireplace will help it to draw better. Lastly, if the home is less than 25 years old, it may be necessary to open a window. Proper drafting depends on air flow, which may be hindered if the home is sealed too tightly.

Wood burning stoves may seem old-fashioned and out-dated, but they are more popular than ever. I find them in quite a few homes that I inspect.

When the cold season arrives, it is sure nice to have a wood burning stove. I can tell you that. A wood burning stove brings back a lot of pleasant memories. I remember loving the smell and the nice heat of our old wood burning stove in our home in Arizona. We had two of them in fact - one in the dining room and one in the family room.

Many people suppose that a wood burning stove is just about the least practical article that a person can install in their home. After all, they think, there are so many disadvantages to a wood burning stove. For example, there is not the same sort of fine temperature control as with a gas heater. Wood burning stoves, basically, are either on or off. When they are on, you constantly have to stock them with wood. When they are off, they take many hours to heat up again.

Nonetheless, the wood burning stove has a lot going for it. Not only can you use it to heat a room, you can also use it to dry clothes, and warm cold feet. You can even cook certain things on some wood burning stoves! I used to love how a big pot of pinto beans turned out after simmering on top of the wood stove all day. There is also the matter of the cost of heating. They are made to burn wood very slowly, and in some places in our area fire wood is accessible at very little cost. Hundreds and hundreds of dollars can be saved every winter if you have a wood burning stove. For many families, that is no laughing matter.

But there are risks associated with wood burning stoves. Although they are not difficult to maintain, they have dangers that regular gas furnaces don't have. Wood burning stoves need to be located in the room in plain sight, not hidden like a furnace. That means that people, and especially young kids, are at risk of burning themselves! Also, the stove pipe should be cleaned now and then to eliminate any buildup which might be flammable. Ask a chimney sweep for advice on how often your stove pipe/chimney needs to be cleaned.

A couple of words of caution: Don't use bricks or rocks to replace a stove's broken leg. And if the glass in the door is cracked or missing then please have it replaced. Also, don't use the stove as an incinerator and be sure the damper works properly. If you move into a home that has a wood stove and you have never owned or operated one then please have a wood stove tech come out to your home and educate you on the proper operation and maintenance of the stove.

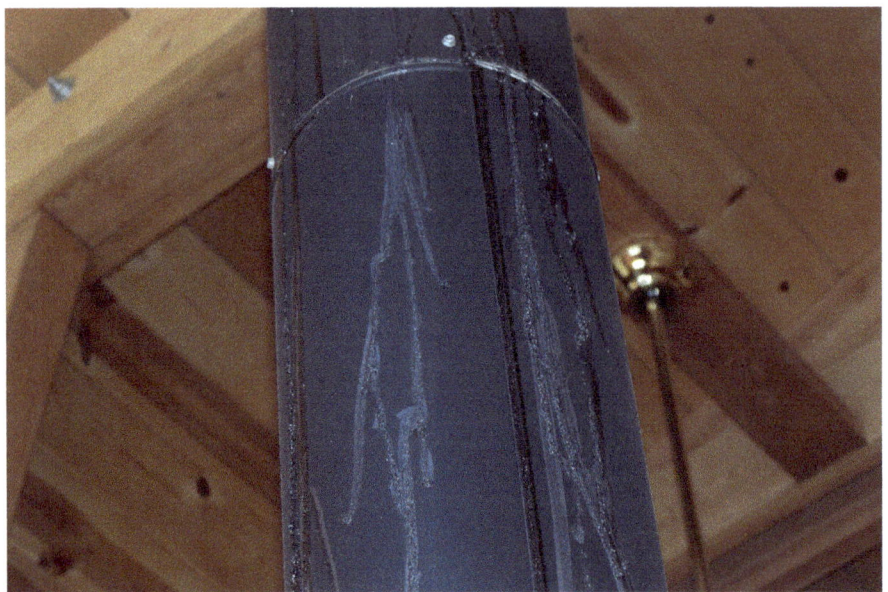

Creosote on the exterior of a stove pipe. Creosote is flammable.

A wood stove can be a real joy to have in the home and, like the fireplace hearth, the warmth it provides can become a memory you will cherish for years to come. Not everyone would agree, however. The other side of the issue is that wood stoves contribute to air pollution.

Our neighbors to the north suffer from poor air quality, especially during the typical wintertime temperature inversions. Studies have shown that emissions from wood stoves add to the problem. Other contributors are vehicle exhaust, industrial sources and smaller commercial businesses such as dry cleaners, gas stations, and water treatment facilities. Some people are calling for changes, such as a ban on wood burning stoves, which they hope will improve air quality with time. They say it's a problem that affects everyone and it will take the efforts of everyone to turn it around. As my readers pointed out, Southern Utahns would do well to take note and make smart decisions with the future in mind, so we will always have our fine, clear air and beautiful landscape to enjoy.

Fortunately, there are those who are taking air pollution seriously and developing products which are designed to still provide the benefits consumers enjoy without adding negative side effects. High efficiency, EPA-approved wood burning stoves are one such product. The newer models differ drastically from the older styles which came before.

Evaporative coolers, heat pumps, air conditioning, central heating, and wood burning stoves are all examples of heating and cooling systems homeowners might choose. Regular maintenance and inspections of these components of a home will help ensure that they will perform adequately and last longer. A qualified professional can do the work for homeowners who are not confident about doing it themselves.

Section 6.4: Structure

Picture this: you are tucked comfortably in your bed at night, sleeping soundly, when suddenly you are awakened. What woke you? You listen intently and hear creaking. Is it the wind? A burglar? No, it's your home "breathing" and in response to moisture and temperature changes.

The majority of the noises are normal and expected in a home. Unless you see walls starting to tilt, doors that won't operate properly, or floors that sag, they are not a reason for concern. The cause of these noises is the normal expansion and contraction of the building materials of which your home is made.

The components most likely to cause noises are wood framing, vinyl and metal siding, plumbing, and heating ducts. As the moisture content in a wood member changes with the seasons it can shrink ¼" or more across 6" of wood grain. This movement makes the various components move against one another making a creaking or cracking sound.

The drywall attached to the wood framing has to adjust to allow for the moving wood. Because of this you may hear cracks and pops. Sometimes nails even "pop" out from the surface of the drywall due to the flexing of the wood behind.

Brick chimneys, the clay liners inside, and the wood framing to which they are attached all expand and contract at different rates resulting in groaning or tinkling sounds. Consider how much the clay liner must move inside the cold chimney as it is heated by a fire below.

Your home likely has metal heating ducts and metal plumbing pipes attached to wood framing. As the metal is heated by hot air or water, it expands and bumps and slides along the wood framing until the increase is accommodated.

Vinyl siding is often an offender for surprising noises on a home's exterior. Vinyl siding is meant to be installed to allow for horizontal movement. As outdoor temperatures rise or in direct sunlight on a cold day, those clicks and thumps may be evident.

Aluminum siding, metal gutters and downspouts, and metal flashing also move when the temperature changes and you may hear the result of that movement.

In fact, everything in your home that is hot or cold, dry, or moist, that moves water or air can cause noises. In most cases, don't worry about it. It's just your living, breathing home talking to you.

Basement, Crawlspace, Foundation

Concrete, in various applications, is seen in just about every home I inspect. One thing I find now and then when doing a home inspection is cracks in the concrete. Concrete cracks in the driveway, sidewalks, garage floor, and unfinished basement floor are most common.

Occasionally, a buyer will ask me whether the cracks are a concern. My first response usually is, "There are three characteristics of concrete: it is usually gray, it gets hard and it cracks." It is practically impossible to determine when a crack occurred in concrete and if it will get larger and cause damage. A visual inspection is usually not sufficient to

Concrete cracked after floor was painted.

determine why they happened either. As an inspector I can only look for indicators that might point to the timing of the crack's appearance. For example, if the garage floor has been painted and there are cracks in the floor but no paint inside the crack then I can deduce that the crack happened after the floor was painted but when exactly was that? Possibly the owners can tell when the floor was painted but I can't.

Sealing a crack with a proper concrete sealant is advised for just about any crack to keep out water that could cause damage to the concrete due to freeze/thaw cycles or to water undermining the concrete. To determine the proper way to seal a concrete crack ask a local concrete contractor to tell you what best works for the size and placement of the crack you are talking about.

The worst crack I have ever seen was in a vacant home, the wall to wall carpet had been removed and the concrete slab was cracked from one end of the home all of the way to the other. The crack was about ¼ inch wide with a raised lip of about 1/8 inch and the depth was deeper than 4 inches. The buyers took my advice and hired a professional concrete contractor to evaluate it. The crack was able to be repaired, the lip was ground flush and the slab was pronounced repaired and in good shape.

A young couple came up to me as I was getting into my truck one day. They had a new home and a few questions had arisen. Their top concern was the basement floor – it was cracked in several places. "Is this a serious problem?" they asked. "What should we do?"

At that point I had a few questions for them. "Is one side of the crack higher than the other? Do the two sides still line up? How wide is the gap?" Generally what I tell clients is that if the concrete crack does not have a raised lip on one side, the jagged points of the crack all line up, and the crack is not wider than 1/16 of an inch, then most likely the crack is not a concern. If the crack has a raised lip, enough to cause a person to trip over it, or the irregularities are not aligned then the crack may have been caused by settling or movement and a professional contractor should be asked to evaluate and advise on the crack.

If a crack is monitored and over time it does not change, it may be surmised that it is not likely to change in the future. However, if movement is observed over time, then it would be prudent to try to determine the cause of the crack with help from an experienced contractor.

An excess of moisture can be the cause of problems, as can a lack of moisture. The overabundance of water can be from rain, the soil or sprinklers, for example. Sprinklers seem to be the largest problem. Having sprinklers improperly adjusted and allowing the water to constantly wet the concrete walls is an easy fix, simply have the sprinklers readjusted. Rain on the other hand is out of our control, except for the addition of awnings and such. Moisture in the soil against a retaining wall will tend to leach through the wall and most likely will leave signs of efflorescence or water stains behind.

Sometimes in a basement or concrete floor signs of efflorescence may be seen. To see efflorescence on a basement wall is not really a red flag. It just means that at some time some moisture has been present. Have the efflorescence cleaned off and then monitor this area over several months and see if any new efflorescence reappears. If so then you might want a contractor to take a look and see if it is serious enough to require taking action. Corrective action to the efflorescence may be to rethink your landscape and watering system. Plants or flower beds along the house, lawn up against or close to the foundation, a water feature near your home - any of these items could be the source of the moisture and cause of efflorescence in the basement.

A crawl space, as the name implies, is a space which is not high enough to stand up in. The term usually refers to the space beneath a house which often has a dirt floor, although some are concrete. Crawl spaces may provide access for maintenance to the electrical, plumbing, heating, and ventilation and air conditioning (HVAC) systems located below the first floor. Other small spaces, such as under the stairs or a tiny attic-like space, are sometimes called crawl spaces as well. But crawlspace in a home inspector's vocabulary means under the house.

Building codes for crawl spaces often specify that the height must be 36 inches where you gain access, but many are less. Some are entirely inaccessible. A space which does not have mechanical services requires only a twelve inch clearance according to many codes. This makes it difficult when structural inspection or repairs are needed.

Crawl spaces can go uninspected for long periods due to the difficulty of accessing them. Poor lighting is another factor affecting the crawl space inspection. Where moisture levels are high for extended periods, structural damage due to rot and termite activity can go unnoticed when crawl spaces are not monitored or carefully examined.

Ventilation of the crawl space is a controversial topic. Industry experts say that "traditionally, crawl spaces were ventilated, or unsealed, so that flowing air would prevent buildup of humidity." However, ventilation allows cool air to flow under the home, which can increase energy use to heat the home and thus increased energy costs. Another concern is that ventilation will not provide further dryness if the air outside is not drier than the air in the crawl space. For instance, in a humid climate in summertime. Many professionals, as well as the U.S. Department of Energy, now recommend that the crawl space be unventilated, or sealed, to prevent these issues and increase energy efficiency."

Homeowners with crawlspaces should inspect them at least twice a year. Be sure to check for moisture accumulation or condensation on any of the surfaces. Your inspection should include the following areas:

1. Cracks in the foundation or structural issues. Cracks that show movement over time, are wider than ¼ inch, or offset should be evaluated by a foundation professional.

2. Leaking foundations. When surface water isn't directed away from the foundation of the home, it can find its way into the crawl space leading to problems such as rot, mold, mildew or insects.

3. Leaky pipes. Check for damaged flooring beneath bathrooms and kitchens.

4. Floor framing, support, and subfloor issues. The members providing support to the home should all be intact and in good condition.

5. Vermin. Destructive ants, termites, or other wood destroying insects and rodents can live undetected under the home for years. Regular inspections can spot them before the problems they cause become severe.

If, when you examine the crawl space, you find potential problems or are unsure of something you find, call in a professional to help with the evaluation.

In parts of the country where basements are found, it's pretty common for the walls to be constructed of concrete block, or poured concrete. Less frequently, I have found preserved wood foundations also known as a Permanent Wood Foundation or PWF.

As the name implies, in a PWF, the foundation walls are made of wood, but it's not just a matter of replacing the concrete walls with wood. The entire design of the foundation focuses on keeping water away from the foundation with gravel, free-draining soil, waterproofing, etc. That helps to maintain the condition of the higher grade treated wood and prevents a damp basement which is a common occurrence with concrete walls.

Preserved wood foundations have been around since the 60s, but it wasn't until the 70s that they really caught on. They have several advantages: they tend to be drier due to the special design features and as a result they are also warmer than a concrete basement. Wood is a better insulator than concrete too. Further, they are easier to finish out. It's a simple matter to insulate, just use batts like with the walls on the above ground levels and you can actually end up with more liveable area because the finish material can be affixed directly to the foundation wall. Another plus is how they accommodate design flexibility.

While PWFs are easy to install, one of the disadvantages is that they must be constructed by competent builders who understand the importance of properly preparing the base layer under the floor, handling pressure treated wood, using correct fasteners, drainage design unique to PWFs, and sealing requirements. When these issues are addressed, a wood foundation will perform adequately and without many of the problems that can plague concrete basements and crawl spaces.

Guidelines, rules for building or codes, apply to every part of a structure. A home inspection is not a code inspection, but there is some overlap. Codes often deal with safety issues which do come under the jurisdiction of a home inspection.

Remodeling jobs often involve surprises. Suppose you want to add an element to your home that will require running electrical wiring perpendicular to several joists. How do you know where to drill the holes? What are the guidelines on hole placement?

A floor joist spans the distance between two walls, a beam and a wall, or two beams. It is intended to support a load pressing down on it. The pressure will be greatest in the middle of the span. This means that the lower edge is being stretched while the upper edge is being squished. The correct engineering terms are tension and compression, but it means the same thing.

When you cut away at the top or bottom edge of a structural member, you greatly reduce its strength. And if you cut in the wrong place or make the notch too big, the joist can become bouncy or saggy. Or, at the very worst, the cut section will become an easy place for the joist to crack or fail completely. You are better off drilling holes closer to the middle of your joists, to preserve the structural integrity of the members.

The code requirements are pretty specific and will help ensure that your floor stays solid. There are different sets of rules depending on the type of joists in the home. Many homes have solid wood 2x8s, 2x10s or 2x12s. Newer homes may have engineered wood I-joists or the less common open web or floor truss joists.

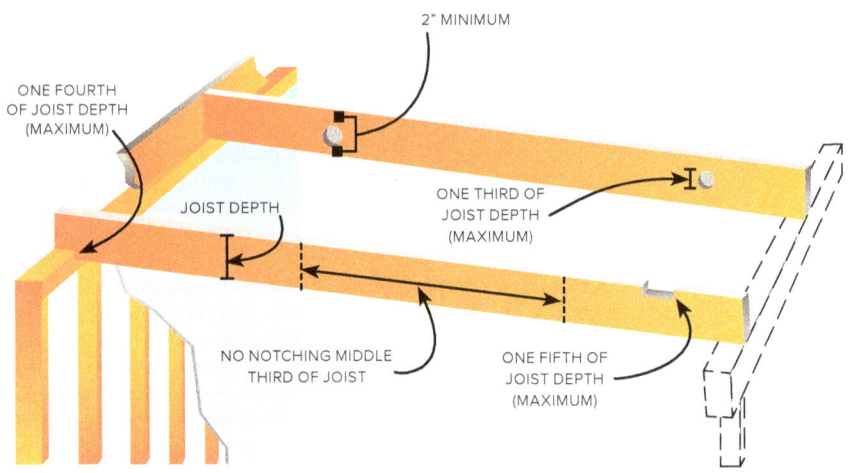

Joist notching and boring guide.

The requirements for the solid wood joists are the most complicated and can be lengthy to explain. In this case, a picture is worth a thousand words. Generally though, notches must be limited to 1/6 to 1/4 of the joist depth depending on the location on the joist. No notches are allowed in the center third of the span. Make sure the notch length is not more than 1/3 of the joist depth. Holes must be at least 2" from the top or bottom edges of the joist. Maximum hole size is 1/3 of the joist depth.

For boring an engineered wood I-joist, ask the supplier to provide you with a set of hole-drilling standards to follow or use pre-drilled knock-outs if they are provided. Notches are not allowed, EVER.

The floor truss joist rules are the simplest – no notching or drilling anywhere. But since the design is an open web, this is not usually necessary anyway since the spaces between the web members provide ample options for cables or pipes.

CHAPTER 6: COMPONENTS OF AN AVERAGE HOME

Cutting through a joist destroys its ability to perform as intended.

Even with such specific guidelines to follow, I have, at times, seen situations when they were ignored. Most often a plumber is the culprit, but do-it-yourself homeowner projects rank a close second. As a home inspector, I will bring to a buyer's attention obvious violations of these rules and then recommend further evaluation by someone more specialized. Consulting a structural engineer or the local building code official, who will have the final say on what is or is not allowed, can dispel any doubts.

What holds a house up, its structure, is an integral and important system of the home. During a home inspection, most of the structure cannot be inspected since it is hidden. However, sometimes visible indicators such as cracks can give clues to the condition of the structure. A home's integrity depends on the foundation and framing of a home, made up of a variety of materials working together to support themselves along with the non-structural components including the building envelope.

Section 6.5: Building Envelope

The barrier between indoors and outdoors, the building envelope, consists of the roof, exterior walls, windows, doors, and floors.

Roof and Attic

Your home's roof is one of its most important components. Proper installation and maintenance will allow the roof to perform its function of keeping out the sun, rain, and other elements. An improper installation or neglected maintenance will affect other components of the home and repairs can be costly.

There are several types of roofing materials and each has its pros and cons. The most commonly found types in our area are tile, metal and asphalt shingle roofs. Built up or flat roofs are less common. Besides being made from different materials, each type also has a different life expectancy. No matter the basic material, all roofs need to be kept free of debris such as leaves and dirt. Keeping the roof clear not only allows the roofing materials to perform the way they were designed, it makes the house look better. An annual inspection of the roof is also an important part of maintenance.

Roof tile has been a major component of building throughout history, from thousands of years ago in China to present day. Travel anywhere throughout Europe, the Middle East, South America, and find beautiful tile roofs that have lasted the test of time. These roofs, found in almost any climate or region, are extremely durable, and as such will protect buildings from some of the most hazardous weather conditions – many times lasting longer than the buildings they protect. That protection is what makes tile one of the most appealing options for roofing material as is evident in Southwest Utah.

During my time as a home inspector, I was inspecting a home in St. George that had a concrete tile roof. I found eight broken tiles so I recommended that a roofer replace them. The home buyer asked a common question, "Why do they break?"

The exact cause of broken roofing tiles can be difficult to determine. If someone walked on the roof, for example installing a satellite dish, or repairing flashing, or cleaning debris off the roof, without knowing how to do it properly they could have broken the tiles. To walk on a concrete tile roof a person should stay on the lower third of each tile where their weight is transferred straight onto the roof deck. Avoid stepping on the cut tiles found on hips or valleys. Walk softly and wear soft flat sole shoes if possible. Other reasons tiles may break is if they were not properly installed or if they had small cracks to begin with or if foreign objects hit the roof such as golf balls, tree limbs, or kids throwing rocks or balls up on the roof, but I think the most likely cause is someone walking on the roof.

A number of years ago while inspecting a two story four-plex property I opened an upstairs bedroom window to look at the concrete tile roof and saw a row of shattered roofing tiles leading toward the next unit, a tile was broken about every two or three feet. The woman occupying the unit I was inspecting was home so I asked her if she knew anything about these broken tiles. She explained. One night as she

Broken roof tiles.

slept in her bed a man came in through her window. Remember this is on the second floor! She woke up, afraid to find a man standing in her bedroom. The man politely asked if he could use the phone because his wife had locked him out of the house. He had climbed up on the roof to try and get in though their bedroom window but it was locked so he came into this woman's bedroom window. She told the man the phone was downstairs. When he left she locked her bedroom door and used her cell phone to call the police. I asked her if she now locks her window. Her reply? "Yes!"

The next most common question about broken tiles is, "Will they cause a roof leak and how quickly should they be replaced?" There are a variety of underlayments (the 'tar paper') that provide a secondary barrier to the weather. Eventually this tar paper will fail and a roof leak will occur. Those broken tiles should be replaced as soon as possible to keep the rain or other moisture on top of the tiles and to prevent the sun from "cooking the tar out" of the underlayments.

I have seen concrete roofing tiles that have been repaired by gluing the pieces back together. I will call these tiles out in my report and suggest that a qualified roofer evaluate these so-called repairs and advise the home buyer.

"How long will the concrete tile roof last?" is another question asked frequently. Typically a concrete tiled roof, properly installed, should last the homeowner 40-50 years. However, even a concrete tile roof needs to be maintained. Debris should not be allowed to collect on the roof. Flashings in valleys and along the drip edge, around flue pipes, plumbing vent pipes, and such should not be allowed to deteriorate.

At one time I inspected a cabin for a client who asked about the metal roofing. She was unfamiliar with it and wondered about the positive and negative aspects of a home with a metal roof. Fortunately I was able to tell her that there are many more benefits than drawbacks.

Long life expectancy, resistance to hail, wind, insects, rot and fire, light weight, speedy installation, and energy efficiency are some of the positive factors. Negatives include cost, denting, possible trouble matching color, and perhaps noise. Also because metal will expand and contract with the temperature, newer roof products have fastening systems which take that into account. Without that, fasteners may tend to work loose over time.

When properly installed a metal roof can last as long as the house. Durable enough to protect the home from water, wind, and heavy snowfall, they are also low maintenance and not susceptible to insects which could destroy other roof systems. Due to the fact that metal is noncombustible; this roof type receives the highest rating for fire safety. Many manufacturers offer 20 to 50 year warranties.

In terms of load, metal roofing is very light. Compared with tile or concrete tile which weighs 750 to 900 pounds per square (an area equal to 100 square feet) or asphalt shingles which weigh in at about 240 to 400 pounds, metal weighs a mere 50 to 150 pounds per square depending on the type of metal used. Because of this, metal roofing may be applied over an existing roof saving the time and expense of a "tear-off." Also, since the metal comes in large sheets it is quicker and easier to install than other types of roofing which must be installed one small piece at a time.

Metal roofs have the added advantage of reflecting the sun's radiant heat. Keeping the attic cooler in this fashion may also reflect a savings in the homeowner's bank account due to lower air conditioning costs.

The biggest drawback with metal roofing is the cost which will be roughly equivalent to other premium roofing products. But since the roof may never need to be replaced during the life of the home, it pays for itself over time.

One of the properties of metal is that it is malleable or bendable if hit with enough force. So it is possible that a metal roof could be dented if hit hard enough with a golf ball or with a large enough hailstone. A loose piece of roofing could also be caught and bent by a very strong wind. In that case replacing the damaged section is more than just a simple repair since the whole sheet would need to be changed out.

An additional concern people may have with a metal roof is the possibility of noise. Won't it be noisy in a rainstorm? Yes, it would if all you had covering the home was the metal. However, the metal will likely be attached to some type of roof decking and if the attic is also insulated, the noise will be deadened further. My own home has a metal roof and excessive noise has never been a problem. In fact we may not even know that it is raining unless we see the lightning and hear the thunder because the sound of raindrops is so muted.

One other factor that could become an issue if the home is added onto could be matching the color of the roof. If the roof has been exposed to the sun for a number of years, the color could have been altered and it may be difficult to match a new roof to an old one. This would also apply to situations when a section of the roof needs to be replaced due to damage.

Having satisfied my client's curiosity about metal roofs, I ascended my ladder to take a closer look at her roof. But since metal roofs are slippery, wet or dry, I did not out climb onto it. Instead, I did as thorough a check as I could from the roof edge and with binoculars. This cabin roof checked out fine.

The most common roof covering material in America is asphalt shingles. They are comprised of a base made of fiberglass, a coating of asphalt and a surface covering of granules. The felt base material gives the shingle its strength while the asphalt enhances its ability to resist weathering and damage. The surface granules protect the shingle from the rays of the sun and provide color.

Asphalt shingles generally have a life expectancy of fifteen to twenty years. A number of factors will influence how long a shingle roof will actually last.

- Thickness – A thicker material will be likely to last longer.
- Color – lighter colored shingles tend to reflect sunlight rather than to absorb it leading to longer life.
- Roof Slope – a more steeply pitched roof sheds moisture more quickly than a gently pitched roof and will last longer.
- Sunlight – the more exposure a roof has to direct ultraviolet light the shorter its life expectancy.
- Ventilation – a properly ventilated attic space increases the life of asphalt shingles by keeping them adequately cooled on the underside.
- Climate – A harsh, moist, cold environment tends to wear asphalt shingles out prematurely.

Defects observable by home inspectors checking an asphalt shingle roof can be grouped into five main categories. This list does not include defects due to inappropriate storage before installation, improper installation, or manufacturing deficiencies.

Cracking, splitting, or tearing is the most common type of flaw observed. A number of conditions cause cracking. One reason might be that the shingle base material is thin. Another reason could be that the adhesive on the backs of the shingle tabs is too strong thus making the roof surface one big membrane without the ability to expand and contract as needed with temperature changes. Also, in areas where large temperature swings occur, cracking tends to be more prevalent.

Another deficiency is cupping which is when the corners of the shingles curve upward forming almost a u-shape. This is one of the signs of an old and worn roof. The shingles dry out and are very fragile.

Granular loss describes another imperfection. It's natural for some of the granules to be lost, but when the loss is severe, patches of the base material can become exposed and subject to weathering at a faster rate than the rest of the roof.

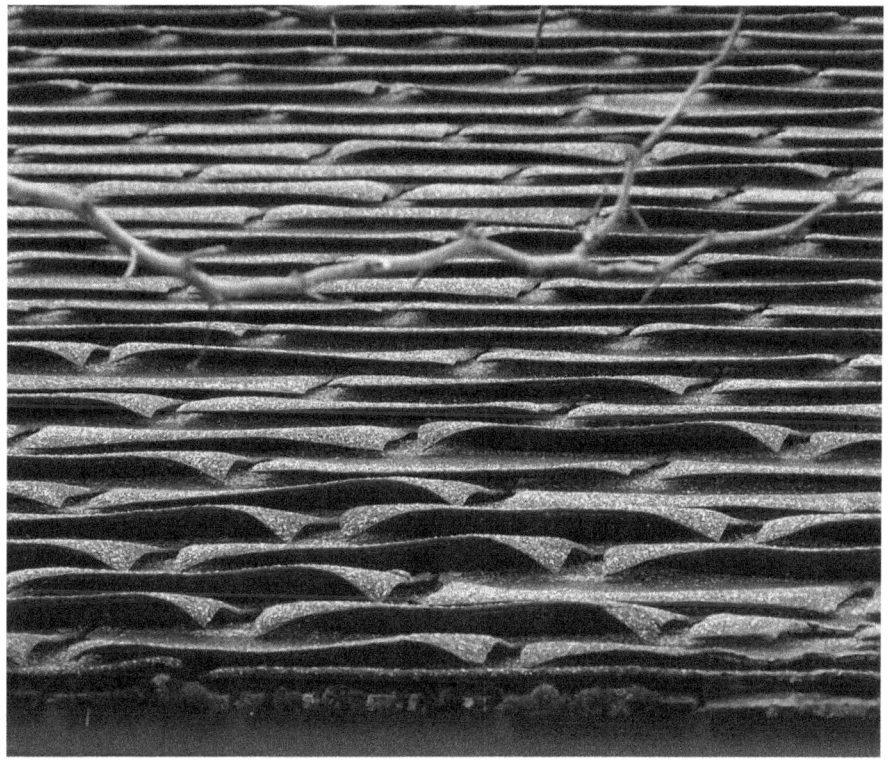

"Fishmouthing" on asphalt shingle roof. Fishmouthing is the opposite of cupping.

Shingles that curl under at the edge of the roof are showing signs of age and wear similar to cupped shingles. As with cupping, the shingles tend to be dried out and fragile. Sometimes a portion of a shingle may curve up at the location of the keyway of the shingle below. This is called fishmouthing since it resembles a fish's open mouth. These raised sections are susceptible to damage and are caused by excessive under-roof moisture such as by a poorly or unvented attic or roof cavity.

In asphalt shingle roof inspections, home inspectors also need to be able to distinguish between normal wear and storm damage.

Residential roofing is typically composed of a variety of materials and surfaces whose main function is to keep out the various elements of weather. The most pervasive and difficult weather element to control is water. Roof flashing is a key feature of roof systems and one of the most important when it comes to preventing water penetration. A primary factor in determining whether or not a roof will leak is the correct installation of flashing material.

Flashing is used to stop water from entering a home at its most vulnerable areas. The most common locations for roof flashing are at valleys, chimneys, roof penetrations, eaves, rakes, skylights, ridges, and at roof-to-wall intersections. Each of these different situations requires a different shape or type of flashing. A few examples are step flashing, kick-out flashing, gutter apron flashing, valley flashing, vent pipe flashing and drip edge.

A sloped roof that meets a vertical wall (like the wall of a dormer window, or where a garage attaches to the two-story section of the house) requires special attention. Step flashing protects the joints between the roof and vertical surfaces. It fits to each course of shingles and looks as if it is stepping up the wall.

Water that travels down the step flashing toward the roof edge should be prevented from entering the wall system with a kick-out flashing. A kick-out flashing, which hangs over the edge of the roof, diverts the water away from the wall and into the gutter. Drip edges are strips that run along the roof's eaves and rakes to prevent water from seeping under the roofing.

Gutter apron flashing is similar to a drip edge. It is placed under the shingles and over the back edge of the gutter to prevent water from running behind the gutters and rotting the fascia.

When two roof planes join together, valley flashing is needed to protect the seam. It has a V or W-shaped channel and is placed on top of building felt, also known as tar paper, before the roof's finish material is installed.

Cone-shaped vent pipe flashing is designed to fit over flues and pipes. A flange at the base is interlocked with the shingles as the roofing is applied.

In general, properly installed flashing will function effectively. However, from time to time, the nails that fasten flashing may work loose, or the flashing material may pull away from seams and joints, and may require maintenance.

Keep in mind that flashing details are a very technical aspect of roof construction, and installation or repair work is best left to experienced professionals. Even an inexperienced homeowner can keep a watchful eye out for potential problems, though. Make a point of checking the roof flashing and the condition of the shingles whenever the gutters are cleaned. Ideally that would be every six months. Look for loose nails and any damage to the seals at the edges of the flashing. Check for exposed joints due to dried out roofing cement which has crumbled away. Also any badly corroded flashing will need to be replaced.

Cold weather brings with it certain difficulties that arise with winter conditions. One such problem is an ice dam. Snow, warm daytime temperatures and freezing nighttime temperatures can create ice

Ice Dam. An ice dam prevents water from running off the roof and may cause it to back up under the shingles causing damage.

build-up in a home's gutters or over the eaves, generating the condition known as an ice dam.

The main cause of ice dams is heat in the attic. Briefly, ice dams form when snow accumulates on the roof. A warm attic causes the snow to melt and run down the roof toward the eaves and gutters. When the melted snow reaches the unheated sections of the roof (eaves and gutters) it refreezes into ice. As freezing temperatures continue, the ice builds up. When it reaches a sufficient height that the melted snow can no longer run off the roof, water may become trapped behind the ice. This is when an ice dam becomes a problem.

The roof covering is designed to shed water toward the eaves and gutters. Shingles, tiles, shakes, etc. are designed for water to run in a downward direction. When an ice dam prevents water from running off the roof, the pool that is formed may actually find its way under the shingles or tiles to a place where water is not supposed to be. Once under the roof covering, the water may penetrate the wall or ceiling structure causing further problems.

Before the snow flies is the time to prepare a "cold roof" by making the attic side of the roof surfaces the same temperature as the exterior surfaces. Generally, this will require the help of a professional (particularly in an existing home), and involves a two-step approach: insulating and ventilating. The end goal is to reduce contact of heated-air with the roof surface which in turn reduces the possibility of melting snow in contact with the roof surface.

Be sure to check that the gutters are not set too high. It's when gutters fill with ice that water is forced to back up under the roofing. Additionally, gutters can be pulled off or damaged by the ice. Gutter guards can be helpful since their purpose is to prevent leaves from clogging the gutters, while still allowing rainwater to enter the drainage

Homeowner solution to an ice dam. Caulking has been applied along the edges of the shingles in an attempt to prevent water from entering.

system. In certain situations, it is better not to use gutters, as long as the water coming off the roof is adequately directed away from the foundation of the house.

Lastly, address any roof leaks immediately. Delaying repair could mean the difference between a minor fix and hundreds, or even thousands, of dollars in required restoration.

A roof can fail as a result of numerous causes. Inadequate ventilation, a common one, can be easily remedied or prevented. A thorough inspection of the roof and attic reveals the current state of these components. Homeowners can then determine what measures, if any, would be necessary to lengthen the life of the roof.

Many homes in the United States were built without adequate ventilation. Homes in our southwest Utah area are no exception. Just the other day a new home I inspected was found not to have any provision for ventilation at all.

Proper ventilation is a consideration many homeowners overlook when adding ceiling and attic insulation. I have found gable end vents blocked off by well-intentioned homeowners trying to keep the cold air out. Their main concern may be to reduce energy costs and all too often insulation is installed over existing soffit or gable vents reducing or eliminating the movement of air. Lack of air flow can lead to trouble.

Without the air flow created by good cross ventilation, hot, moist air becomes trapped in the attic. With changes in temperature, the moisture condenses and saturates the roof decking - the plywood or other sheet material installed over the trusses that makes up the primary support surface for the roof covering. Condensation causes the deck to rot, warp, delaminate, and deteriorate, a condition which often goes unnoticed until the roof begins to leak or the inspector falls through during an inspection. Moisture can also saturate the insulation causing it to become matted down and somewhat less effective. A few times I have found the bathroom exhaust venting into the attic, thus adding moisture to the area. I have also seen buckets and cans in the attic catching water from roof leaks.

Another problem results from the trapped hot air. Elevated temperatures in the attic can cause asphalt shingle roofs to cook causing them to crack, curl and warp. The resulting life expectancy of the roof is reduced dramatically. Excessive heat also dries out the wood structure and can force air conditioning systems to work overtime.

A common belief is that a system containing soffit and ridge vents should be employed because it will draw air across the entire underside of the roof deck. Both types of vents are easily blocked either by insulation, as mentioned above, or snow or debris rendering them useless. A better system for pitched roofs with open soffits is soffit screens installed every eight feet combined with dormer vents out of sight on the back side of the house.

If you need to have a leak repaired or add attic vents, please hire a professional roofer that will do the job properly. One summer I "added" an attic vent while at an inspection. I was walking on an asphalt shingle roof, and in the blink of an eye my left leg went through the roof all the way up to my hip and gave me one doozy of a bruise. The shingles had been repaired at one time with silicon seal where they had been leaking but the silicon seal hadn't completely stopped the leak and continued moisture intrusion rotted that section of the roof.

My inspection of the attic interior showed the roof sheathing to be so rotten it was just hanging together by a thread in the area where my leg went through the roof. I included digital photographs of the hole in the roof from both the inside and outside in my report to the buyer. I also shared the photos with the homeowner. She had a roofer on site in less than an hour and he confirmed that the roof leak had never been repaired but simply patched.

Generally, ventilation recommendations (which are by shingle manufacturers, local building officials, and roofing product dealers) should be considered and implemented. Whenever in doubt, seek the advice of a professional.

One of the notations clients find regularly in a home inspection report is the depth and type of insulation in a home. I also comment when no insulation is present. However, I do not provide an R value because there are so many factors which impact that number (more on that below). At times a certificate listing the R value of the insulation can be found attached to a roof truss in the attic by the insulation installers. If I find this I note it in the home inspection report for the client's information with a qualifying statement that I do not verify the accuracy of it. Buyers generally want to know about insulation because it gives them an idea of the R value available and thus the energy efficiency of the home.

R value is an indication of a material's resistance to heat flow. With regard to insulation, the higher the number the greater the insulating capacity. Now and then I meet a buyer who makes a comment such as, "R-35 is that all? Back in Wisconsin we always had R-50!" or "The garage is not insulated? Back in Maine we always insulated the garage."

In response to these comments I explain to the buyers that R 35-38 is considered normal in most areas of Southwest Utah and that garages are normally not insulated here.

Another area I often find uninsulated is a home's attic access, representing a big source of energy loss. This breach in the attic insulation amplifies heat loss in winter and heat gain in summer. In addition, such accesses are typically not sealed properly. Estimates are that a gap of ¼ inch around the perimeter of the access hatch can leak roughly the same amount of air supplied by a typical bedroom heating duct.

Since various types of insulation are made of different materials and have distinct density and thickness, R value varies from type to type. Kinds of insulation include blankets in the form of batts or rolls, blown-in loose-fill, foam insulation, rigid insulation, and reflective systems or radiant barriers.

The overall R value of a wall, ceiling, or floor will also vary depending on how the insulation is installed. When calculating the R value in a multi-layered situation such as a wall or ceiling, the R values of the individual components are added together.

However, insulation which has been compressed will not provide the full insulative protection described by the associated R value. This can happen, for example, if a heavier type of insulation is installed over a lighter insulation in an attic, or if batt insulation made for a certain wall thickness is crammed into a smaller space than intended. This can also happen if someone walks through the attic stepping on the insulation as they go. This is one reason that I only walk in attics where walk boards are provided.

Another consideration is thermal bridging. This occurs, for example, when batt insulation is installed between joists and refers to the heat that is transferred by the joists themselves. Metal framing has a much lower R value than wood framing.

When considering what type of insulation is best, the US Department of Energy states that the answer depends on:

- how much insulation is needed,
- the accessibility of the insulation location,
- the space available for the insulation,
- local availability and price of insulation, and
- other considerations unique to each purchaser.

The best way to decide is to compare products using equal R values. Also be sure to read the labels. The R value should be clearly stated. The label will also contain information on the suitability of the product for various situations, and statements about health, safety and fire-hazard issues.

The Department of Energy has a handy zip code based insulation program which can provide helpful information for decision making. The site includes an insulation fact sheet and a diagram showing where homes should be insulated. To learn more about insulating a home, this page is a good place to start.

Attic access pull-down stairs are a convenient way for homeowners to, what else, access their attic and open up additional storage space in a home. Although the concept is simple, the installation of this type of stair unit according to the manufacturer's instructions will actually be an advanced level do-it-yourself project best left to professionals.

CHAPTER 6: COMPONENTS OF AN AVERAGE HOME

Attic pull down stairs installation instruction. Note the screw placed where a nail should be.

Even with the detailed directions that are provided with each unit, home inspectors tend to agree that the majority of attic pull-down stairs, whether installed by homeowners or professionals, are installed incorrectly.

The most common deficiencies observed are:

- Improper nails or screws. I often see drywall or deck screws used, not the proper 16d nails or 1/4"x3" lag screws. The stair maker specifies a certain type of fastener for a reason, probably related to safety. Some screws intended for other purposes may have reduced shear strength because of how they were made so they won't hold up to the pressure put on them by pull-down stairs.
- Improper nailing pattern. Many times manufacturers will have a sticker saying "PUT NAIL HERE" to guide installers who then ignore it. Again, the nailing pattern is engineered for safety.

- Legs not cut properly. Legs need to be cut at the right angle as well as the right length. Attic pull-down stairs are actually a type of ladder and should be as solid as a ladder before use.
- Frame not headed off properly. The opening in the ceiling must be strong enough to properly support the load. Most attic stairs are made to fit between joists in which case strengthening the opening is fairly simple. In situations where the stair runs perpendicular to the joists, special consideration needs to be taken when framing the opening.
- Gaps at hinges. This is usually an indication that the stairs have been cut to the wrong length. The legs should not be too long or too short. Legs too long will not allow the stair to extend properly, while legs too short put too much weight on the ceiling end of the stair for safe use.
- Loose mounting bolts. This is a problem not so much related to installation as it is to age. But if a stair was improperly installed in the first place, then loose mounting bolts may be likely to occur sooner.
- Lack of insulation. Hatches in many houses (especially older ones) are not likely to be insulated and/or weather-stripped. An uninsulated attic hatch freely allows attic air into the home which may cause the heating or cooling system to run overtime (this does not apply to an attic that has been finished and made part of the living space or to a hatch located in a vented garage).

Much of what a home inspection covers is related to safety issues. This is especially true with attic pull-down stairs. Here's a quote from the Louisville Ladder Installation Instructions: "Improper installation of this folding attic ladder could put undue stress on its components and could result in failure and serious bodily injury." The deficiencies discussed above might seem like small issues, but as I've said before, "It's only a small thing until someone gets hurt."

Cladding

The exterior walls, the vertical portion of the building envelope, are covered by a protective, weather-proof layer which is referred to as cladding. Similar to the roof, the purpose of the cladding is to keep the wind, rain and other weather elements outside the home. Again, like roofing, there are many different types with diverse properties.

When aluminum siding was introduced in the 1940s, it had many advantages to offer homeowners. As an affordable choice, it gained popularity in the 1970s. Although its usage is now in decline, it is still a common cladding material.

Aluminum siding is manufactured from sheets of aluminum which are formed and then chemically coated with a protective layer. Paint is then applied to further protect the surface and to add color. The siding is then baked to make the finish even more durable. Some types of siding have a texture added also.

Ornamental panels on the Chrysler Building and the Empire State Building in the 1920s demonstrate some of the first uses of aluminum for building. After World War II, with an abundance of aluminum available, manufacturers began to suggest uses for the metal that included siding for homes. It had many advantages to offer over other materials typical of the time. By the 1970s, aluminum siding use began to decline mostly because it takes a lot of energy to produce. Less expensive alternatives, such as vinyl siding, started to be developed.

Advantages of aluminum siding include its durability. It won't rust so it lasts a long time (perhaps for the life of the building) with proper care. It accepts paint well and comes in a wide variety of colors and textures. It's lightweight and easy to handle. It is fireproof and waterproof. And lastly, it's recyclable.

On the other hand, although it accepts paint well, it DOES need to be painted every 5 to 10 years, a process which can require extensive preparation. Additionally, it can dent fairly easily and may be difficult to repair, but insulated types makes dents less common. Scratches show up well too, especially when the bare metal is exposed. Even though it does not rust, it can be stained by rust on adjacent materials and the nails which secure it to the wall can corrode. Also, some people feel that the sound of rain or hail on the siding is just too noisy.

Made of PVC, or poly vinyl chloride, vinyl siding is a popular alternative to aluminum siding. Commercial production of vinyl siding began in the 1930s. It's manufactured using an extrusion process in which several layers are bonded together. The color is integrated into the material.

One of the reasons for its popularity is the relatively low cost. It's a good choice for homeowners with a smaller budget. Color choices are varied with up to 350 different, long-lasting options. In addition to color choice, homeowners can choose from several different textures and styles. Vinyl siding is relatively easy to install and maintain. Most of the time, it just needs to be washed every now and then. Lasting up to 25 years, it is not susceptible to damage from bugs or rot.

Nothing is perfect and vinyl siding is no exception. For example, over the long life of the siding, the color may fade a bit making it

CHAPTER 6: COMPONENTS OF AN AVERAGE HOME

Melted vinyl siding. Very likely the BBQ was too close to the wall.

impossible to match if repairs are needed. Extreme weather or other sources of impact can cause it to break, crack, dent, warp, or melt. Lastly, it is not water tight. It's possible, under the right conditions, for water to find its way between the sections of siding and cause damage to the surfaces underneath.

Another of the many options for cladding a home's exterior walls is wood siding. It was one of the first methods available and as such has timeless, classic appeal. Since it can be installed vertically or horizontally, it can suit many styles of homes.

Wood siding is a generic term for a variety of shapes or profiles made of wood, including log siding. One of the advantages of wood or log siding is its insulative value. The material adds to the R value of the exterior walls. It is also durable when diligence is practiced in maintaining its condition.

On the downside, wood siding is susceptible to harm from insects. In damp climates, it may also be damaged by mold. As mentioned previously, maintenance is a key component in prolonging its life. If that is ignored, the wood may dry out and crack. Extreme weather conditions could negatively impact the siding as well. Lastly, it tends to be more expensive than other cladding choices.

Traditionally, stucco consists of cement, lime and silica applied in several layers over lath of wood or metal. There are other methods, but this is the technique that has been around the longest. When applied in this way, the stucco basically creates a thin, concrete shell around a home.

Similar to other cladding choices, stucco has good insulative value. Not only does that help with energy costs, it also reduces sound transmission. By nature, stucco is also fire retardant, and not susceptible to bugs, rot or mold. The components which make up this type of coating are also long lasting, when properly applied, stucco may last perhaps fifty to eighty years.

Initially, the cost to install may be relatively high. But when spread across the likely lengthy life, the cost is reasonable. Additionally, since the cost of maintenance and effort required is low, stucco becomes even more appealing. It resists moisture well, but tends to crack, a condition which is more cosmetic than structural.

Stucco may be painted, but it's generally not recommended. One reason is that the paint must be removed prior to any repairs or refinishing. Also, stucco is supposed to breathe to function properly and paint can impair that.

Masonry is a popular choice for chimneys and decorative features on homes. Some homes are built with the façade entirely of brick. Concrete block fences are common as well. No matter the setting, brick or stone projects a feeling of permanence and stability.

Generally, masonry as a building material includes brick, concrete block or stone. There are also manufactured stone alternatives and other products which fit under the category of masonry. All of these are installed using mortar to hold the units (pre-cast or natural) in place. When properly installed, masonry components will last a lifetime or longer, especially with regular maintenance.

The mortar is probably the most vulnerable part of a masonry installation, especially when not properly mixed in the first place. Mortar is prone to water damage and can eventually wear away. Homeowners need to constantly monitor the mortar to be sure it is performing as intended.

It may be necessary at some point to have the mortar "repointed" especially when large holes or washed out sections appear. Repointing involves replacing damaged or deteriorated mortar between the brick, stone, or block. Note that it's critical that the old mortar be replaced with mortar of equivalent strength, composition, and appearance. This keeps the masonry uniform and keeps the base materials from cracking. If the old mortar is replaced with a stronger mixture, the masonry won't be able to breathe with the natural freeze/thaw cycles.

The brittle nature of masonry makes is susceptible to cracks. While major cracks that leave big gaps may indicate serious structural issues, minor cracks can and should be mended. Left unrepaired, a more serious and more expensive problem may result.

Chimney needing repointing.

Water is masonry's worst enemy and it is expected that water will soak into it occasionally, but it is not supposed to reach the interior and damage the structure behind the masonry. Discoloration can be an indication that water is getting in. Water that penetrates the brick or stone can also cause it to crack as a result of the freeze/thaw cycles. Protect the masonry by directing water away from the home. Homeowners should also see that appropriate flashing is installed and that it remains in proper working order. The same goes for the chimney cap.

Homeowners also need to keep an eye on joints between masonry and other surfaces, such as around windows and doors. With time, the caulking sealing these joints may deteriorate allowing water a point of access. When this occurs new caulking is needed.

CHAPTER 6: COMPONENTS OF AN AVERAGE HOME

In the case of brick or stone, it may be tempting to apply a sealant to keep moisture out. Unfortunately these sealants, which create a continuous barrier on the surface, also trap moisture inside. With time they can acquire a cloudy appearance and may contribute to spalling (flaking of the masonry surface) in colder climates. A better choice is a water repellent which works by penetrating the surface of the brick or stone perhaps as much as 3/8 inch. Since it doesn't seal the surface, but instead helps it to shed water more effectively, the brick and mortar are still able to breathe and adjust to temperature changes as needed. It's my understanding that these guidelines do not apply to concrete blocks which typically need to be sealed or painted every three to five years.

Efflorescence is a common occurrence on new brick or stonework. Dissolved minerals, which are part of the makeup of the masonry, are

Efflorescence. The white, powdery minerals on the surface of the concrete block are drawn out by prolonged wetness.

released by water which carries them to the surface. The water then evaporates leaving behind a white, powdery substance. These white stains are mainly a cosmetic problem and will eventually subside if left alone. However, water chronically entering the masonry could cause problems over time.

Homeowners should clean masonry only when necessary, taking care to be gentle. Improper cleaning methods can easily damage the surface. Contacting a local contractor in this field of expertise is recommended before you go any farther with this project than brushing off the efflorescence and possibly correcting sprinklers that are wetting the masonry. As with any home project, some things are best left with the experts.

Windows and Doors

Windows and doors aren't just holes in the walls. From windows we can observe the sunsets, children laughing and playing, and traffic driving by. Doors allow us to come and go. In interacting with windows and doors, safety must be a priority.

It's the sort of thing that happens in the movies. The hero crashes through a window which breaks into dangerous shards, yet he escapes without injury. The reality is a little different. Many years ago when my younger sister and brother were children, they were chasing each other through the house. Accidentally, my sister crashed into the glass in the front door. The impact of her fist caused the glass to break and seriously cut her wrist taking quite a few stitches to repair the wound.

Incidents like this one were probably the impetus for the implementation of standards regarding safety glazing. In 1977, the Consumer

Product Safety Commission (CPSC) established a federal safety glazing standard (Code of Federal Regulations (CFR) 1201, category II) designed to reduce the risk of serious injuries caused by accidental impact with glazing materials in homes and other buildings. The standard was intended to apply to all glazing materials, and preempt local building codes which varied in degrees from location to location. At about the same time the American National Standards Institute developed its standard referred to as ANSI Z97.1. The ANSI Z 97.1 standard is most commonly used for residential applications while the CPSC CFR 1201 is more often found in commercial applications for glazing.

According to the Federal safety glazing law, defined hazardous locations within architectural applications (homes and buildings) must use safety glazing. Generally the list of hazardous locations includes "doors intended for human passage, windows within 24 inches of a door, bath and shower enclosures, glazing adjacent to passages where there are walking surfaces adjacent to the glass and the bottom edge of the glass is within 18 inches of the floor" and all other areas where human impact is likely. Various local code authorities may have additional requirements in addition to the minimum standard defined by the Federal law. Overhead glazing such as that used for skylights must meet requirements for safety specified by local building codes.

Safety glazing prevents windows from shattering into shards of glass. Instead, if a fully tempered pane of glass is broken, by a blow, it breaks up into relatively small pieces which greatly reduces the chance of serious injury in comparison with ordinary glass. Likewise, when laminated safety glass is broken the pieces stick to the plastic inner layer, again reducing the likelihood of injury.

Be aware that safety glazing is not required for all windows and doors in a home, just those in potentially hazardous locations. So impact accidents causing glass to break into shards can still occur and often do occur. The Consumer Product Safety Commission reported that in 1995, there were over 225,000 glass related accidents in the U.S. These statistics were gathered from the emergency rooms of hospitals and doctors throughout the nation. That number is estimated to be higher now especially with the increased use of glass in building features. Also, many more incidents go unreported.

Typically safety glass, as defined by the Glazing Association of North America, is tempered (specially heat-treated), or laminated with a plastic layer between two panes of glass, or contains wire embedded in the glass. The wire embedded glass is considered safety glass only in certain applications. To identify safety glass, look for a permanent mark, commonly known in the industry as a "bug", in one of the corners showing the manufacturer's name, type of safety glass, and the thickness.

Along the same lines as the standards regarding safety glass, the International Residential Code requires that all bedrooms have at least one egress window, defined as a window large enough to allow occupants to escape in the event of a fire, or to allow a fully equipped firefighter to enter from the outside. The requirement pertains to windows installed in finished basements as well as those in bedrooms. The way out that is normally used, the basement stairs or the hallway, could very easily be blocked by flames or thick, black smoke. In such a situation windows that are large enough to allow occupants to exit the home, or firefighters to enter, become essential lifesaving features.

Properly installed and maintained smoke detectors are important safety devices, but being able to leave the home once they've gone off is even more important. This is especially true for upstairs bedrooms and basements, where the stairway is often the only escape route. If that stairway is blocked and the windows are too small for a person to fit through, you can be trapped.

Local regulations vary, so before remodeling it's a good idea to verify the standards for your area. In general, egress windows must 1) have a minimum net clear opening of 5.7 sq. ft. Net clear opening refers to the actual free and clear space that exists when the window is open. It is not the rough opening size or the glass panel size or any other size, but the actual opening a person can crawl through, 2) The opening height must be at least 24 in., and the opening width must be at least 20 in. Keep in mind that a window opening that's the bare minimum of 24 in. high and 20 in. wide does not meet egress requirements, since its net clear opening is only 3.33 sq. ft. A window has to be taller and/or wider than these minimums to meet the 5.7-sq.-ft.-opening requirement. 3) The bottom of the clear opening must be within 44 in. of the floor. 4) The window or other opening must be operational from the inside without keys or tools. Bars, grilles and grates over windows must be operational without tools or keys and still allow the minimum clear opening.

New homes built to code should have the proper size basement and bedroom egress windows. But if you live in an older home, especially one that has been remodeled or added onto, you may need to double check that the window size is adequate for your family's safety. Using a tape measure, note the width and the height of the fully opened window. Multiply the width by the height of the opening to determine whether it's the required 5.7 sq. ft., or 821 sq. in.

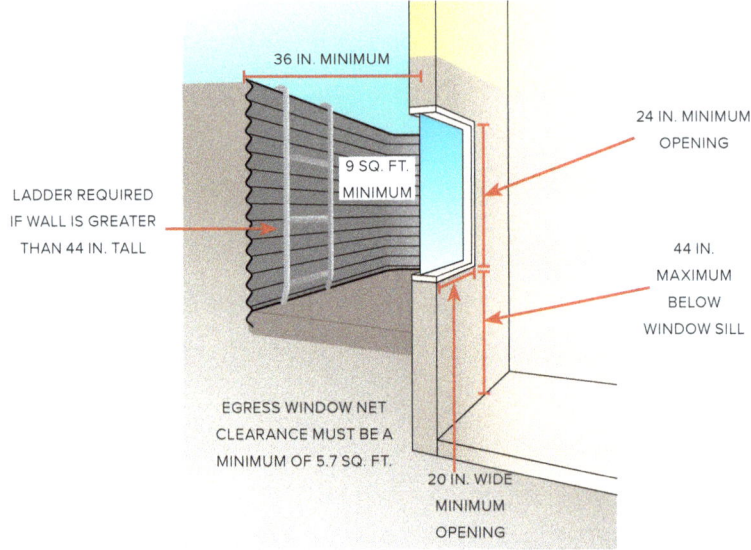

Egress window specifications. Egress windows allow occupants to exit a home's basement in case other exits are blocked by fire.

Some older homes I inspect were built before there were any egress window requirements. Also, these requirements have changed over time and I see many homes that were built when the egress window standard was smaller than what is required today. Many times an attic or basement in a newer home was legally remodeled into a family room or office which didn't require egress windows. Subsequently these spaces may have been converted into bedrooms which do require them. As part of remodeling projects, homeowners may unwittingly replace large egress windows with smaller, non-egress windows.

Not all basement rooms need a legal egress window, but they're a must for basement bedrooms. When basement rooms are converted into bedrooms without the knowledge of code inspectors and without the requisite egress window, they create a treacherous fire trap. Some may think they can call a given room a den before the inspection and a bedroom after in order to get around the requirement. Code inspectors, however, will consider any bedroom-sized room with a closet a bedroom, no matter what the blueprint says.

Basement fires are common, so this is really more than a code issue. And of course, what's good for you will be good for any other owner of the home as well. While you may not fully recover what you invest in the larger egress windows should you sell the home, in the meantime, you will have the added assurance that your family has a way out should the need arise.

A cheerful fire on a cold winter night is, well, pleasant. But when the fire is not planned and not in the fireplace, it is very dangerous, maybe even deadly. Garage fires can be especially perilous since it is more likely for them to go unnoticed for longer than a house fire. Due to the flammable and burnable materials that people often store in their garages the fire may spread more quickly, and even explosively, to the house. This is one of the main reasons that building codes require the separation between a house and garage to be fire-resistant.

What constitutes fire-resistant construction? According to the International Building Code, a fire resistance rating describes "the period of time a building or building component maintains the ability to confine a fire or continues to perform a given structural function or both, as determined by tests prescribed in Section 703." Simply put, fire-resistant materials are intended to restrict the spread of fire for a period of time, giving the occupants time to escape the building.

Local code enforcement organizations have the final say on the specifics of what is allowed in construction. However, the following offers some general guidelines based on the International Building Code (IBC) and the Universal Building Code (UBC).

- The wall separating the garage from the house must have ½-inch thick gypsum board on the garage side. The UBC specifies the use of Type X gypsum board, as well as fire tape to seal joints on drywall and gypsum board. According to Underwriters Laboratories testing, a wall assembly with Type X gypsum board on both sides sealed with fire-tape is assigned a one-hour rating.
- If there is any habitable space above the garage, or if the attic over the garage is not separated from the attic of the house, 5/8-inch Type X gypsum board is required on the garage ceiling. In addition, all of the supporting walls need to be clad with 1/2-inch gypsum board. The UBC requires a fire-rated floor-to-ceiling assembly.
- There should not be any opening for air duct systems in the garage, such as returns or vents. These might actually fuel a fire or allow the fire to spread more easily. Any ducts passing through the garage or penetrating its walls or ceilings are required to be a minimum of 26-gauge sheet steel or other material approved by the Authority Having Jurisdiction over code compliance in a specific location. Penetrations of drywall are then required to be sealed with approved firestop caulking. A rare exception I have seen is the use of a fusible link louvered opening - when the fusible link melts due to excess heat the spring loaded louvers close automatically.
- The floor of the garage must be noncombustible (carpeted garage floors are not approved as they could be a fire hazard) and slope toward a vehicle door or floor drain.

CHAPTER 6: COMPONENTS OF AN AVERAGE HOME

A pet door in a garage door nullifies the fire-resistance of the door.

- The entry into the house from the garage must have a 20-minute-rated fire door with a self-closing mechanism, a minimum 1-3/8-inch thick solid wood or steel door. The UBC additionally requires the door to be self-closing and self-latching. I commonly find either the latch or the closer not functioning on these doors, especially in new construction. Workers will often disable these features so that it's easier for them to enter and exit and then forget that they have done so. Another situation I have seen is pet doors cut through the door. While this may allow convenient access to the garage from the house for pets it, unfortunately, nullifies the fire-resistance of the door.

One of the simplest things homeowners can do to prevent a garage fire is to keep the area clean and organized. Flammable items kept in the garage should be stored properly. It is a good idea to get rid of unneeded items (flammable or not) before they become piles of junk (i.e. fuel for a fire). Trash cans kept in the garage should be emptied regularly since household trash is full of flammables. Regular removal of dust, cobwebs, and trash, which burn readily, will aid prevention efforts.

Finally, increase the likelihood of detecting a garage fire by installing a smoke detector. As with all smoke detectors in the home, check how it's functioning at least once a month. Additionally, it's a good idea to keep a fire extinguisher in a handy location, for fires either in the garage or in the home.

Safety in the garage extends to the garage door and the automatic opener, a couple of the most commonly overlooked maintenance items in the home and frequently noted as safety defects in a home inspection report. Due to the size and weight of the overhead garage door, it could quite possibly be the largest moving component in a home. As with the rest of the home, it requires regular maintenance to keep it in safe working order.

How does it work? We don't tend to think much about how it works unless it's not functioning properly. Since it is so large, a garage door may use one of a couple of different methods for making it possible for a person to open. A properly balanced door should be able to be lifted to a half open position and balanced there. One system for balancing overhead garage doors could be a combination of pulleys and weights. This is usually found in older doors.

Nowadays most doors have a system of springs under high tension that help balance the weight of the door. Sometimes these springs fail, and when they do the flying pieces of metal could cause serious damage. For this reason it's important for the spring system to incorporate some way of preventing this possibility – sometimes a cable runs down the middle of the springs, holding it in place should it break. If you are uncertain about whether your door includes these safety features, have it examined by a garage door specialist. Working on the spring system yourself could be very dangerous.

Many garages also have automatic garage door openers. By itself, the opener is not strong enough to lift the door. It works in tandem with the balancing system described above – another reason to keep it in good repair.

When a large and heavy component such as the overhead garage door is not properly adjusted, it can pose a serious safety risk, not only to a vehicle, but to a person, especially a small child, or to a pet. As such, certain safety features have become required. These basic safety characteristics on your garage door should be periodically tested, ideally once a month.

One of the traits to which I am referring is the automatic reverse. Modern doors are designed to stop closing and reverse to open when they meet an obstruction. Doors manufactured prior to 1982 may stop, but not reverse and should be upgraded. A good way to test this feature is to place a roll of paper towel on its side on the floor where the center of the door will be when the door closes. The door should reverse and reopen when it comes into contact with the roll. If it doesn't, a professional should be consulted to remedy the defect as soon as possible.

The electric eyes are another way the automatic reverse feature could be triggered. Properly mounted, the eyes should be facing each other

Electric eyes trigger a closing garage door to reverse if something crosses their path.

five or six inches above the floor on either side of the garage door frame. When the beam between the eyes is interrupted while the door is in motion downward, the door should immediately reverse. Again, if this feature isn't working as intended, it should be repaired without delay.

Since the garage door opener is powered by electricity, it won't work during a power failure. It should have an emergency release, usually a short rope, which disengages the opener from the door when pulled. This allows a person to open the door manually. It's a good idea to know where this is located and how to operate it, just in case.

A couple of final comments about the garage door opener – it's like a key to your garage. Just as you would change other locks or keys in the home when you first move in, change the code for the garage door opener and its remote control. Also, make sure children understand that the garage door is not a toy. Do not allow them to play with it or the remote and for their safety, make sure the control pad is mounted at least five feet above the ground.

This has been a brief discussion of various aspects, conditions and systems in the typical home. I've also mentioned quite a bit about the importance of safety and how technology and science have been able to improve the quality and safety of our lives. Each day I go out to inspect homes, I see areas of improvement – changes that have been made over time as our body of knowledge increases. For example, people used to build homes with knob and tube wiring (and the copper wiring was insulated with cloth). They didn't know that grounding the system would improve safety. To take it a step further, breakers are the advanced version of fuses and GFCI outlets are an improvement on those. Homes used to have lead or galvanized pipes too. Even lead paint was considered desirable due to its durability. Asbestos products were used extensively in homes because they are highly-effective, inexpensive and resistant to fire. Single paned windows have been upgraded too. I could go on, but you get the idea.

With all the changes that have occurred over the last several decades I have to wonder what the future holds. What features, materials and systems will the home of tomorrow contain? What will we know then that transforms what we believe to be true today? And how will that alter the future of home inspection?

Part 3: This and That

Chapter 7: Maintenance Tips

While it is true that home inspectors mostly work for home buyers, home inspectors have a set of skills that can be useful for homeowners as well. They also know a bit about health and safety issues that might be of concern to buyers or sellers. Additionally, their constant experience with homes also means they can offer practical maintenance tips, give words of advice and act as a resource for their community.

Section 7.1: Landscape Drainage

One time when I inspected a fairly new home, I found that around the rear and west side of the home the soil had settled some next to the foundation thus forming several depressions which would collect water. Also two downspouts were missing and one rain gutter was damaged.

In order to reduce the chance of water intrusion into a home or a basement the first order of business should be to correct the soil grading around the home and install proper gutters and downspouts with the downspouts draining water at least six feet away from the home.

Occasionally, I have seen houses that are not provided with rain gutters and downspouts so the water flows right off the roof onto the ground. I can mention two reasons why this is not a good idea. First, the water may tend to collect near the home and, second, the splashing water can often cause stains on the exterior finish of the home.

No gutters and downspouts. Notice the channel carved in the dirt due to water running directly off the roof.

Not only does water end up on your property from rain directly, but also from runoff from the roof of the house. A gutter/downspouts system helps channel the water a safe distance from the structure. The roof water runs into the gutters which are connected to the leader drains - the vertical pipes on the outside of your house that link the gutters to the downspouts. The downspouts then direct the water away from the house.

Where the water flows on the rest of the property also needs to be taken into consideration. Landscape drainage can be handled in a few different ways. One of the most important things is to be sure that the surface adjacent to the house all slope away from it. Another technique that can be used is to create swales. A swale is a channel which directs water away from the home. It can be a subtle way of directing the water flow.

In some cases it might be appropriate to install a lawn drain, perforated pipe or drain tile, a catch basin or french drain. All of these will collect surface water which then enters an underground pipe leading to a desirable area for discharge.

After a hard rain take a few minutes to walk around your home. Look for pooling water and maybe even take a few photos of any pools of water you may find. Contact a landscape company to evaluate your yard and photos so they can give you some advice on how best to reduce or eliminate standing or pooling water by your home. Thus helping to prevent water intrusion or damage.

Section 7.2: Plants and the Home

Included in a thorough home inspection are the trees, vines and bushes growing around the outside of a home and the effect they have on the home.

Trees are valuable items to have around. Not only do they bring shade and song birds, but they may even provide fruit. On occasion, however, a tree may cause damage to a home. Trees growing too close to a house pose the greatest threat. Movement by branches in contact with a roof could cause harm. A tree does not stand still like a statue but moves in even the gentlest breeze and in SW Utah we get some mighty strong breezes at times! A severe storm could cause large limbs to break from a tree and fall on the roof causing damage. I have seen roofs where asphalt shingles were pried off long ago by tree limbs exposing the bare wood sheathing to weather. In many cases the impairment goes unnoticed since the tree branches also hide the destruction they cause.

Plants too close to the house.

Fascia boards, the trim along the edge of the roof, have been rubbed by branches until only a minimum of material remains. At one inspection I observed a small tree branch coming up through the flashing around a chimney! A tree with branches growing over a chimney can cause a chimney not to draw properly. Trees also have leaves or needles which can fill up rain gutters and down spouts. Leaves and needles also tend to pile up in roof valleys and can cause a roof to drain improperly. A tree can also cause havoc with overhead electric service lines. In such a case the electric power company should be asked for advice.

A tree too close to the house may also tend to send roots toward the foundation which may negatively impact the home. Roots can also cause problems for sewer lines and sidewalks and can be a cause for concern for driveways as well.

Ivy or vines growing up walls or the chimney of a home may look pleasant and give the home some character but the problem is what may not be visible. The vines or ivy can hide pests such as bees, wasps, mice, termites, or ants. The vines also physically attach themselves to the house and this can cause damage to the exterior siding, brick, or wood. Vines have been seen to grow up into the eaves and into the attic. I observed some vines in an attic over twenty feet long and still growing! Additionally, I have seen vines actually growing over and under concrete tiles on a roof extending from one side of the roof to the other.

Bushes and shrubs along the foundation of a house are said to soften hard edges and add beauty with blooming flowers and sweet scents. But once again these bushes and shrubs tend to hide problems such as foundation cracks, rotten wood siding, cracks in stucco and brick homes, termite tubes, ants and more. Additionally, these plants require water to keep them growing and healthy. It is not a good idea to keep the soil around a foundation too moist yet many homeowners install watering sprinklers and bubblers for their foundation plantings to water them. At the same time the water is soaking the foundation of their home. Many, many times I have seen water damage from this kind of watering.

Damage to stucco walls from sprinkler located in the corner.

Even a low water, desert type of planting needs consideration. Although the plants in a desert landscape take less water, if they are too close to the house they can tend to hide problems as well. It's not uncommon for me to see homes where piles of dirt have been hauled in then shaped into rolling hills and mounds. When this soil is actually up against the home, often a stucco home, it can hide pests and problems just as the plants would.

The idea is to think smart. Look closely at the trees, bushes, vines and shrubs and consider what they could be hiding. Then decide if they should be pruned or removed. As a certified home inspector I made suggestions for buyers and homeowners to consider regarding the vegetation around the home. But, ultimately the final decision was theirs.

Section 7.3: Regular Maintenance

Whenever I celebrate my birthday the occasion reminds me, oddly enough, to change the batteries in my smoke detectors. Birthdays, anniversaries, the change of the seasons, the New Year, the time change – these are all good reminders of maintenance items that ought to be taken care of periodically.

Clogged dryer vent.

CHAPTER 7: MAINTENANCE TIPS

Once a year, like your birthday or anniversary or the beginning or end of summer, consider having a professional check your heating or cooling system to ensure optimal performance or make repairs as needed. Clean your ducts to better your heating system's efficiency as well as to reduce household dust. Check for leaks around the joints of the ducts. Clean your thermostat's heat sensor and contact points. Call a professional to inspect and clean your chimney. Do a quick visual check to make sure gutters are clear. Neglected gutters can lead to wood rot problems, pest infestations, wet basements, foundation damage and many other expensive complications. Change the batteries in all the smoke and carbon monoxide detectors.

Clean exhaust fans and vents in the bathrooms and kitchen. Ensure that window wells are free of debris and draining properly. Cut back any tree limbs or shrubs that could damage the home. Don't forget to clear the dryer vent. Also, check over the water heater for any signs of corrosion or leaking.

A couple of times a year, like the first days of Spring and Fall or when the time changes, check ceiling and surfaces around windows for evidence of moisture.

Inspect caulking around showers, bathtubs, sinks, and toilet base. Look up at ceiling areas beneath bathrooms for signs of leakage. Check all faucets, hose bibs, and supply valves for leakage. Do a quick visual review of the basement and/or crawlspace for moisture or leaks. Examine all wood surfaces for weathering and paint failure. Decks, patios, porches, stairs, and railings should be inspected for deterioration and repaired as needed. Attend to any missing, loose or damaged roof shingles or tiles (check for open seams, blisters, or bald areas on flat roofs). Make sure downspouts divert water away from the foundation. Check the attic for evidence of leaks. Look over flashing around all surface projections, sidewalls, and protrusions.

Take time to observe whether the fascia and soffits have deteriorated or become damaged.

Once a month, like the first or last day or the 15th, test batteries of smoke, heat and carbon monoxide detectors. GFCI and AFCI outlets and breakers also need to be tested each month. Clean or change furnace filters every thirty days during times of use.

Home maintenance is one tradition that all homeowners should keep, and inspectors advise homeowners not to skip or put off important repairs. Not only does regular upkeep on a home help the home retain its value, but it also makes it more pleasant to live in a home where all the systems are functioning as they should.

Section 7.4: First Impressions

It is commonly said that you only get one chance to make a first impression. Within the first few seconds of meeting someone, people pass judgment. Regardless of how much you say or how you say it, the first twenty seconds are all it takes for people to decide what kind of person you are. It is human nature to constantly make these appraisals, in business and social environments. And once made, first impressions are virtually unchangeable.

CHAPTER 7: MAINTENANCE TIPS

This evaluation process occurs in every new situation including when buyers meet a house for the first time. Curb appeal is a major factor in the first impression of a home. If the exterior looks neglected, a potential buyer will likely assume that there are other things neglected as well, and may not even come inside.

Most homeowners are under the impression that the only time to have an inspection done is if you're buying or selling a home. Conscientious sellers might consider having a home inspection done prior to listing the home as a way to detect maintenance issues or needed repair projects. A seller then has the option of either fixing the problem or using the report as a tool in negotiations with potential buyers. As a homeowner, when you consider the investment you have made in purchasing your new home, a professional home inspection is comparatively inexpensive.

It might seem kind of backwards for a home seller to hire a home inspector. Most people probably consider that the responsibility of the buyer, not the seller. But having a home inspected prior to listing it is a very smart strategy. The inspection report will point out trouble spots to the homeowner and give them an opportunity to fix them before putting the home on the market.

Like real estate agents, a home inspector also has the opportunity to view a large number of homes. What I saw when I first pulled up to a home gave me a pretty good indication of what I would see inside and if excessive clutter and a larger number of defects, either major or minor, would lengthen the inspection process. A basic home inspection takes into account deferred maintenance items such as peeling paint on exterior door trim or broken roof tiles or loose deck railings. Since these things can lead to major damage to the structure of the home or represent a safety hazard they are noted in the report.

Simple improvements that anyone can do include applying a fresh coat of paint to siding, doors and trim. Paint is one of the most affordable home improvement products around. And it can make a huge difference in the way the front door, for example, is perceived. Further, if there are any cracks in the driveways or walkways, I recommend sealing them. Make sure all railings are tight and secure. Also, make sure that the home has sufficient lighting, and that all of the light bulbs are working.

Some improvements may be more costly, but well worth the effort. For example, broken windows ought to be replaced. Also, make sure to take a look at the roof. In some cases it makes up about 40 to 60 percent of the exterior view of a house. Damaged shingles and missing or cracked tiles are a very common problem. Repairing the roof covering before major problems develop is much less costly than replacing the entire roof and any resulting interior harm.

Other things that homeowners can do to upgrade the exterior look of the home include keeping bushes attractively trimmed, mowing and edging the lawn in summer or shoveling the walk in winter, and making sure the yard is tidy.

The best possible first impression catches the attention of potential buyers. On the other hand, once a poor impression is made it's almost impossible to alter it. An appealing first impression in a home can be the tipping point that makes a potential buyer want to stop and view a home instead of driving on by.

Chapter 8: Termite Facts

Termites. Just the mention of the word is enough to cause some people to roll their eyes and groan while others shudder in disgust. The name termite comes from the Latin word for woodworm – a very appropriate name since termites feed primarily on wood and other dead plant material, more specifically the cellulose fiber of plants.

What this means for homeowners or homebuyers is that any house constructed of wood components on the interior or exterior is susceptible to infestation from termites or other wood-destroying insects. Once inside a home, termites might feed not only on wood, but also on paper, books, cloth, cabinets and carpets.

Termites prefer to remain within their ideal environment, tending to stay hidden in tunnels in earth or wood or in tubes of their own making. For this reason, their presence often goes unnoticed until it becomes obvious.

Telltale signs of termite infestation include mud tubes, swarms, or damaged wood members. Mud tubes are usually about the size of a pencil and connect the colony to infested wood. They may be visible on a concrete foundation or hidden behind siding. I have seen them lining the walls and hanging from the ceiling of a little used storage room.

Evidence of termite activity. Subterranean termites build tubes in order to move from place to place without being exposed.

Spring is the time of year that large numbers of winged termites emerge from their protected environment. Triggered by warmer temperatures and a more abundant water supply, they swarm to disperse and begin new colonies (some types of ants also do this and may be easily confused with termites due to their similarity in appearance). Once on the ground, they shed their wings and pair off. Fortunately few of these winged termites, which are incapable of eating wood, survive exposure. The remains of a swarm are best removed with a vacuum; however a swarm does indicate a more serious infestation which should not be ignored.

CHAPTER 8: TERMITE FACTS

Termite-damaged wood is usually hollowed out along the grain with bits of dried mud or soil lining the tunnel. Wood damaged by water or other wood destroying insects will not have this appearance. However, infestation may not be evident because termites tend to leave the outer surface of a wood member intact. Discovery of hollowed wood may happen only by accident such as if a vacuum cleaner bumps into a baseboard revealing the damage behind.

Confirmation of the presence of termites is best done by an experienced termite inspector or a licensed pest control company. A termite inspector visually checks over the home for the presence of termite damage or evidence of past treatment for termites. A termite inspection report does not, however, guarantee that a home is free of termites because the inspector only reports on what he can see. Things such as stored items in closets, under cabinets, firewood stored along the side of the house or garage, tools and such make it impossible for a termite inspector to see every inch of the home and some evidence of termites may not be found until the spring cleaning urge hits a person who cleans out the garage, or closets.

Many termite problems can be prevented. The intent of treatment or prevention measures is to create a continuous, impenetrable barrier around the home. This is practically impossible to achieve in real life, however certain actions can make the possibility of a termite infestation less likely.

The following suggestions may help:
- plan a minimum 2-inch clearance between the house and planter boxes or flower beds

- eliminate all wood-to-soil contacts such as trellises, untreated fence posts, and stair case supports (incorporate masonry blocks or treated wood as a base)
- keep shrubs and other plantings trimmed away from the house to help make it easier to inspect the foundation line
- seal openings in the foundation
- remove wood debris or remaining stumps from around foundations
- don't stack firewood along the walls of a house or garage or shed
- in a crawlspace, have at least 12"-18" clearance between floor beams and the soil underneath

Fact Sheets, a Handbook for Homeowners, Ten Termite FAQs and other information are all available online to assist homeowners in breaking down misconceptions about termites.

Chapter 9: Mold Basics

Every home has mold. There are 1.5 million different species. The appearance of mold takes many forms and colors; fuzzy, slimy, fine stringy hairs, cobwebby or powdery coating, or dark stains. It may be green, gray-green, black, white or yellowish in color. It is impossible to identify mold just by looking at it. A lab must test it in order for it to be labeled with confidence.

Any type of mold is harmful if allowed to grow excessively, however, in small quantities, not all types of mold are considered hazardous to a person's health. It's the high concentration of spores in indoor air that leads to mold-related health problems. Spores are the mold's way of reproducing. Like microscopic dandelion seeds, the spores drift through the air until they land on a new surface where they start to grow. To those who are sensitive to mold, inhaling spores can cause health problems such as breathing issues, allergies or asthma. These health problems may be very serious for those individuals with lung disease or weakened immune systems.

Moisture is one requirement for mold growth. When moisture levels in materials remain elevated, such as from a roof leak that goes unrepaired, mold colonies are likely to grow. In order to continue growing, the mold fungi requires: oxygen; a moderate temperature (between approximately 45° F and 85° F); a food source (usually the surface on which it is growing); and moisture. When any of these requirements is not met, mold growth ceases and enters a dormant state. Most are difficult to actually kill.

In the desert climate of Southwest Utah, I find that mold is most likely to be associated with some sort of prior water damage. Once the source of the moisture intrusion is stopped, the mold problem is likely to be solved as well.

If mold is allowed to grow unchecked, it can be hard to get rid of it in a home. Depending on where it is located and how extensive the problem is, it might take a certified professional to remove the mold. Once the situation is resolved, a homeowner would be wise to take preventive measures to ensure that the problem does not happen again.

Chapter 10: Home Repair and Renovation

I inspected homes in Southern Utah for more than a dozen years. A lot of the time the homes I inspected were pretty normal. There might be a couple of things that need attention – broken roofing tiles or a water heater temperature and pressure discharge tube missing or some burned out light bulbs. On occasion I find a more serious defect that translates into a safety hazard – like exposed wiring in the attic or a leaky roof or termites.

In one home I inspected, the owner had installed the kitchen cabinets. For whatever reason, he or she attached 2x4s flat against the wall and then attached the cabinets to the 2x4s. The result of this was that the cabinet fronts were now closer together than they were intended to be and the drawer handles interfere with the opening of the drawers in the corners. Another consequence is that countertop is no longer a standard depth. Not a problem for this homeowner, he or she just installed floor tile for a countertop. The edge was a combination of wood trim and ¼ round plastic.

I have also seen duct tape used for just about everything including patching holes and cracks in the tub. That's very creative but not very durable.

One place I see a lot of surprises are in homeowner-installed bathrooms. Such things as the toilet installed in such a way that the bathroom door won't close, or sinks with automotive radiator hoses twisted in all directions substituting for the drain and trap, or a bathroom shower with the controls for the water in the bedroom on the opposite side of the wall. Once I observed a garden hose run through the crawlspace then up through the floor by the bathtub for water to fill the tub

S Traps are not approved because the water tends to be siphoned from the trap allowing sewer gases to enter the home.

CHAPTER 10: HOME REPAIR AND RENOVATION

(no hot water mind you, just cold). I've also seen water heaters with the water lines hooked up backwards, a toilet hooked up to the hot water instead of cold and a working toilet with the drain pipe not connected to the sewer line but just running outside into a pit behind the house.

Kitchens are fun too. For example, one house had no receptacles in the kitchen so extension cords were used to bring power in from the laundry room. One homeowner mounted wheels on a built-in style dishwasher so it could be used as a portable unit. Another installed a propane RV kitchen stove placed on bricks where a full size stove would be. Lastly, I pitied the homeowner without a kitchen sink; they had to use the sink in the laundry room to wash dishes!

These true examples might be good for a laugh, but I want to point out that although in a lot of places creativity is a good thing, unfortunately home repair isn't one of them. An improperly done job just poses too much of a risk. So where should a homeowner draw the line? When should a professional handle the job? I suggest that most average do-it-yourselfers stay away from electrical, plumbing, roofing and structural work because of the complexity. Be honest with yourself when evaluating your skills. The money saved by doing it yourself is not worth the price you may pay if your family's safety or your home's integrity is compromised, even if unknowingly. If working on your home is a source of pleasure for you, stick to projects within your skill level.

One home improvement project that many homeowners seem to feel confident tackling is building a deck. For many, a deck is an extension of the home. It brings indoor life to the great outdoors. With a little care, a deck can last for many years. Neglected, it can become an eyesore or worse, unsafe!

Most municipalities require a permit to build a deck. The permit process helps to ensure that the deck is safe and sound through verification of the design and inspections of the deck at various phases of construction. Unfortunately, many decks get built without a permit. The result is that many decks are poorly constructed and some are unsafe.

According to researchers at the Wood Materials and Engineering Laboratory at Washington State University, "The deck is the most dangerous part of a house, with more injuries and loss of life than any other part of the home structure." Their research showed that more injuries can be connected to failed decks than to all other wood building components and load situations combined (except for hurricanes and tornadoes).

Many decks fail because they are old, worn and rotted. Others fail because they were not built properly in the first place. The most critical connection is the deck-to-house connection. A good deck-to-house connection incorporates a ledger that is attached securely to the house structure with bolts not nails and includes flashing to keep water from leaking behind the ledger. Joists should attach to the ledger with properly nailed joist hangers.

Guard rails keep people, especially young children, from falling off the deck. Guards are required for decks higher than 30 inches from the ground. In some municipalities, a guard is required for a deck that is 24 inches from the ground. The specifics of a quality guard rail are spelled out in local building codes, but this list will provide some general guidelines:

CHAPTER 10: HOME REPAIR AND RENOVATION

The guard rail should be 36 inches high (a deck over 6 feet high requires a 42 inch guard)

There should be no openings larger than 4 inches so nobody can fall through. It should be strong enough to hold a person that falls heavily into the rail or balusters. It should not be easily climbable – no footholds.

If in doubt, have the deck inspected by a qualified contractor to see that it has been installed properly. More than likely it would be money ahead to have a professional contractor install the deck for you. This way you know it will be installed correctly.

The secret to a deck that looks good over the years is wood sealer. Unsealed wood will absorb water and expand, then dry out and shrink. Over time the wood splits and deteriorates. Here's a test to see if your deck needs sealer. Pour a cup of water onto the wood; if the water beads up and runs off, the deck is in good shape. Otherwise it needs sealer.

With care and attention to proper construction techniques, a deck can last many years and provide a safe place to enjoy the great outdoors.

Chapter 11: Safety and Security

Old houses are generally thought of as continually needing work. They can turn out to be one project after another. Some buyers might be thrilled at the prospect while others would describe the same home as a money pit. Yet people still say, "They don't build 'em like they used to." When it comes to the topic of homes, a great deal has changed over the past hundred or so years.

Today's homes are safer in a number of ways than homes built 30, 50 or even 100 years ago. One example that this is true is in the area of fire safety. Old homes were built of flammable materials, such as wooden strips called lath as the backing for plaster walls, using techniques that didn't impede a fire's progress. Knob-and-tube wiring, which was common in its day, was prone to damage to the wires and easily-overloaded circuits possibly leading to fires. Our modern houses are constructed using fire resistant drywall and current codes specify the use of fire blocking. Better protected wiring also helps keep us safe. Contemporary homes are even required to have smoke detectors which add another measure of protection when properly used.

CHAPTER 11: SAFETY AND SECURITY

While driving to an inspection one day I happened to see a home along the way that had some damage caused by a fire. I began wondering if the home owners had prepared for the possibility of a house fire. Did they have smoke alarms in each bedroom, hallway, and stairway in the home? Did they have a carbon monoxide detector near the bedrooms? I wondered if they had an emergency egress in each of the bedrooms, those upstairs and in the basement.

I questioned where the fire might have started. If it was in the kitchen did the owners have a fire extinguisher handy? Since gasoline, oil and paint are commonly stored in a garage, I wondered if that could have been where the fire started. If so, was the garage ceiling in good shape and void of openings that could have allowed the fire to enter the attic? Was the door from the garage to the home a self-closing fire rated door to help contain the fire in the garage?

You might think it kind of odd for all of these things to pop into my head while driving to an appointment, but I just wondered what happened and if the home owners had their fire safety devices in place and in operational condition.

I guess I will never know the answers to these questions, however if you have any questions about fire safety contact a local home inspector. And, of course, the local fire station stands ready to help you as well. When in doubt about whether your home is fire-safe, please ask the advice of a trained professional.

In a related line of thought, carbon monoxide is another safety concern. Carbon monoxide (CO) is an odorless, colorless gas that can be toxic to humans in high concentrations. It can form when fuels such as natural gas, oil, and propane are burned. Home appliances such as furnaces, water heaters, and stoves can produce this deadly gas. Normally, these appliances are designed to vent the CO to the outside, but sometimes things go wrong. Harmful levels of CO can collect inside a home when there is incomplete combustion of the fuel, the appliance is not properly installed or adjusted, or when there are blockages, leaks or cracks in the venting systems.

Prevention is the key to avoiding carbon monoxide poisoning. There are a number of things homeowners can do. Regular professional inspections of fuel-burning appliances are very important. Since many of these items are furnaces or heaters, the best time for the inspection is prior to the start of the cold weather season. These also include gas dryers, fireplaces, and wood stoves. And when the devices are in use, only the proper fuel should be used.

When potential sources of CO (fuel-burning appliances) are installed or replaced it must be properly done with venting to the outside whenever possible. Of course, installation and any necessary repairs should be performed by a qualified technician.

Gas stoves or ovens are not intended to heat the home, even temporarily, and should never be used for that purpose.

A vehicle idling in an attached garage, even with the door open, is a danger. Fumes can build up very quickly in the garage and living area of the home. This is one reason why a self-closing device on the door between the house and the garage is an important safety feature and a key item that is checked during a home inspection. The door should have a tight seal all the way around to prevent seepage of exhaust or gas fumes.

Consider installing a CO detector to further protect your family. Be sure to follow the manufacturer's instructions for properly locating and installing the alarm. Realize that the alarm should be just a backup, not a replacement, to proper use and maintenance of fuel-burning appliances. Before you buy, do your homework to find the best option. They are not all alike. As with smoke alarms, check the batteries regularly – once or twice a year.

Learn what to do should the CO alarm activate: First verify whether it is the smoke alarm or the CO alarm. Then check if anyone in the home is experiencing symptoms which may include fatigue, dizziness, blurred vision, nausea, or confusion. If so, everyone should leave immediately and seek medical attention. Do not wait or ignore symptoms, especially if more than one person feels them. Loss of consciousness and death may result. If no symptoms are felt, open doors and windows immediately and shut off all fuel-burning devices that may have caused the alarm to activate. Then have a qualified technician inspect your fuel-burning appliances and chimneys to make sure they are operating correctly and that there is nothing blocking the fumes from being vented out of the house.

Years ago while living in Texas, my family and I occupied a mobile home while our house was being built. Our son, then two, began to cry in the early morning hours. My wife woke me and asked me to see what was troubling him. As I opened the door to his bedroom a smell of exhaust fumes about took my breath away. I did not know the cause of the fumes at the time, but saw that my son was not well, somewhat disoriented. Immediately I urged my wife to get the other children out of the house and to open all of the windows and doors. Meanwhile I jumped in the shower with my two year old son in my arms and turned on the cold water. After a few minutes he began to be himself again and I investigated the source of the fumes. It turned out that high winds the previous evening had knocked the gas water heater's flue pipe off allowing the fumes from the water heater to enter the bedroom. When morning arrived I called a plumber and requested that an electric water heater be installed without delay. I fear to think what might have happened if my son's cries had not woken my wife or me.

For more information on how to reduce your risks from CO and other combustion gases and particles or to receive answers to questions you may have regarding Carbon Monoxide visit the EPA's Indoor Air Quality Information website.

Another aspect of safety is home security. Burglars don't just pick locks; they also attack by crowbar, hammer, wrench, saw, and kicking in the door. A deadbolt goes a long way towards foiling them.

During a home inspection I always check the deadbolts on the doors of a home. One thing that I find is that the deadbolt will not extend to its fullest length because the mortise in the door frame is not deep enough. A carpenter could easily correct this problem for the home owner.

The main problem I feel with a deadbolt that doesn't extend fully when the door is shut is the false sense of security it is offering the occupants. When a deadbolt is installed properly it offers many times more security than the ordinary door knob latch and it may also help keep some unwanted visitor out of your home.

If an exterior door doesn't have a deadbolt and a home owner wants the added protection that a deadbolt offers it can be added to most doors. In simple terms this is how a deadbolt is installed. Two holes must be drilled in the door, one for the lock assembly and the other for the cylinder. The strike plate covers a deep hole, called a mortise, in the jamb. The lock will come with paper templates that make drilling easy. Then you just screw everything together. It's a simple job in a wooden or steel door, but if you have any qualms, hire a professional to do the job for you. The cost of a new deadbolt is just pennies compared to what kind of damage an intruder can do to person or property. A note of caution – dual key deadbolts (those which require a key to operate both inside and out) are no longer recommended because in case of emergency you may not be able to find the key to let you out of the home.

Safety is only one way recent homes are better. Another aspect of modern homes is their energy efficiency. We now have better materials and methods for insulating a home. High performance windows with protective coatings and improved frames are also available. Ensuring that the home's "envelope" is free of holes and cracks and that the ducts of the heating and cooling systems are well sealed reduces the likelihood that drafts, moisture, dust, pollen, and noise will enter, making the home more comfortable for the home's occupants. Our lives are made easier through the use of energy efficient appliances and systems.

Many of the components now used in building homes are more durable than those used in the past. For example, copper or PVC plumbing pipes will last a lot longer than the galvanized or lead pipes used previously. Vinyl window frames or siding are also longer lasting than wood, even when the wood has been maintained well.

On the other hand, the individually-built, hand-worked, attention-to-detail oriented owner/builders of history often built with longevity in mind. I've inspected many homes still standing on foundations 100 or more years old. When owners carefully update particularly the plumbing and electrical, these pioneer era houses can very likely provide a sturdy and comfortable home for many more years.

Given that today's homes are superior in a number of ways to yesterday's, why are new houses built to look as if they were old? And what is the appeal to so many people who desire to live in an actual old house even with all its possible problems? Perhaps it has something to do with the human tendency to characterize years gone by as "golden." That can't be the whole story, though. And as the writer Oscar Wilde once wrote, "The one charm of the past is that it is the past."

When people say they don't build houses like they used to, I believe they're not referring to the lumber, pipes and wiring. They're actually referring to the one intangible quality that can't be built into any new house, no matter what the price: the genuine charm of an actual past.

Chapter 12: History of the Home Inspection Report

Many years ago, 1976 to be precise, the American Society of Home Inspectors was founded "to establish and advocate high standards of practice and a strict code of ethics" for member inspectors. This group of inspectors that banded together illustrates the beginning of home inspection as an industry. Prior to this time home inspections were "walk-throughs" with the buyer's real estate agent. Or sometimes a buyer hired a general contractor to look over the home.

Eventually a need for specially trained inspectors, now known as home inspectors, was recognized. Today, the majority of homebuyers (almost 80%) request a home inspection before purchase. As of 2012 there were an estimated 32,500 home inspectors nationwide.

Through the intervening years the inspection report evolved along with the profession. The first home inspection I had was on a home purchased in 1998. The inspector spent about an hour at the home. The report was a single 8-1/2 x 14 page carbonless copy handed to me at the conclusion of the inspection. The content of the report was a series of check boxes and a few handwritten comments. It didn't tell me much that I didn't already know about the home.

I didn't have a home inspected again until 2003. By that time the home inspection industry had progressed, but was still a long way from where it is today. The second report was considerably more detailed. It consisted of four typewritten pages. It covered more systems of the home and in more detail. Although the inspection took only about two hours, it took the inspector several days to complete the report for us. Since we still lived in another state, we received the report by fax.

It was shortly after this experience that I completed my inspection training. Right from the start I used a computer to generate the reports. The software allowed me to enter my findings as I progressed through the three-hour inspection making it possible for me to have a report of 25 or 30 pages ready immediately. I could also include digital photographs which was unique at that time. Many times, though, when clients were unable to attend the inspection, we delivered the report by fax which was still generally more common than email.

Today, computer-generated reports are the industry standard but not all home inspectors are using a computer to generate their report. Various reporting systems are distinguished by the readability of the finished report and assorted other features. Some home inspection reporting software, in my opinion, makes the report hard to read with little icons placed here and there for the reader to decipher. Reports regularly include digital photographs. The use of a computer makes it possible to include more detail more efficiently. And as the use of email grew so did the need to produce the report in a format that is able to be easily emailed or uploaded to a website for review. Another distinguishing feature is the report package. No longer does a buyer receive just a report, but also a "homeowner's manual," a filing system to track home-related expenses such as repairs, utility bills or property taxes, a maintenance schedule, perhaps coupons from vendors to help them repair or furnish their new home, a list of life expectancies for common appliances, and more.

A word of caution when selecting a home inspector. Don't let price be the only consideration. A home inspection should not be considered a commodity. Experience, education, certification and, yes, even the quality of the finished report are all important factors to consider before making a choice. Underlying the technology and other advances is still the simple truth that the report will be only as good as the inspector.

Conclusion

What the Experts say about Home Inspection

If you've been in the market to buy a home, hopefully, you've been informed that it's a good idea to get a home inspection as part of your due diligence. Home inspections are not required as part of the purchase process, but the information gained can help a buyer make a better informed decision and give them peace of mind about what is likely the biggest purchase of their lives. Don't take my word for it, read what the experts have to say about it.

The Department of Housing and Urban Development states, "For your protection, get a home inspection." Why? "Buying a home is one of the most important purchases you will make in your lifetime, so you should be sure that the home you want to buy is in good condition. A home inspection is an evaluation of a home's condition by a trained expert. During a home inspection, a qualified inspector takes an in-depth and impartial look at the property you plan to buy."

According to the American Society of Home Inspectors, "Buying a home could be the largest single investment you will ever make. To minimize unpleasant surprises and unexpected difficulties, you'll want to learn as much as you can about the newly constructed or existing

CONCLUSION

house before you buy it. A home inspection may identify the need for major repairs or builder oversights, as well as the need for maintenance to keep it in good shape. After the inspection, you will know more about the house, which will allow you to make decisions with confidence."

"Home owners cannot afford surprises. Everything may look fine on the surface, but there may be trouble lurking," says Don Crawford, Past President of the National Association of Home Inspectors, Inc. (NAHI). "A qualified home inspector will have the experience and training to provide information that will assist the buyer in making an informed decision. Problems that the seller or the realtor may not be aware of become the financial responsibility of the buyer - if they are not corrected prior to the final sale of the house."

RealtorMag (Official Magazine of the National Association of Realtors) reports, "Before you make your final buying or selling decision, you should have the home inspected by a professional. An inspection can alert you to potential problems with a property and allow you to make an informed decision." Be aware that a home inspection is an evaluation of the home, it is not a guarantee that everything can be found and reported on in the 2-3 hours time the inspector will be at the home. You may find something after you move in that the home inspector did not. A home inspector gives you the best evaluation he can in the time he has to spend on your home.

When buying a home it's easy to get caught up in the excitement of it all and not see the flaws a home might have. My advice? Side with the experts - hire a professional home inspector before you close the deal.

Index

A

air conditioning systems, 11, 16, 17, 64-66, 127
    basic components of, 65
    central, 66
    evaporative cooler, 17, 58-61
    filter, 18-19, 62, 128
    heat pump, 64-66

arc fault circuit interrupter (AFCI), 11, 43-44, 128

American Society of Home Inspectors (ASHI), 6, 149, 152

appraisal, 7, 10

attic, 11, 17, 18, 25, 82
    access, 97, 98-100
    insulation, 94
    leaking, 27, 94, 95
    ventilation, 94

B

basement, 73

    dampness, 75-76

    fire safety, 110-13

    floor and floor joists, 77, 79-81

    foundation, 75-77

    Preserved Wood Foundation (PWF), 78-79

    water seepage, 75, 120-2

bathrooms, 11, 138

    electrical outlets, 41

    toilet, 47-78

C

carbon monoxide (CO), 143-46

central air conditioning system, 64-66

    (see also *air conditioning systems*)

chimneys, 67, 72, 127

    backdraft, 67-68

    creosote/soot, 70

cladding, 72, 101-8

cooling system

    (see *air conditioning*)

crawl space, 11, 17, 23, 73-77

D

decks, 139-41

    guardrails, 140-41

    joist supports, 140

do it yourself (DIY)

    (see *maintenance*)

doors

    exterior, 18, 21, 146

    metal clad insulated, 11

    pet, 115

drainage, 11, 76, 77, 107, 120

E

efflorescence, 75-76, 107-8

egress windows, 110-13

electrical outlets, 38, 44-46

electrical system, 11, 16, 38-47

    arc fault circuit interrupter (AFCI), 11, 43-44, 128

    fans, 46-47

    fuses and circuit breakers, 23, 38

    ground fault circuit interrupter (GFCI), 11, 20-21, 41-43, 128

    grounding, 40

    outlets (receptacles), 38, 44-46

    panel, 11, 28, 38

F

fans, 46-47

fireplaces, 66-68
    creosote/soot, 70

forced air heating system, 62-66
    filter, 18, 62, 128

flashing, 72, 85, 90-91, 128

foundation, 11, 17, 73, 124, 127
    cracks, 73-75
    settlement, 75

furnaces, 17, 62

G

garages, 18
    door photoelectric eye, 117
    doors, 11, 116-18
    electricity, 42, 118
    fire and health hazards, 113-16, 142
    general consideration, 143

glass, safety, 108-10

ground fault circuit interrupters (GFCI), 11, 20, 41-43, 128, 150

ground water
    (see *drainage*)

gutters and downspouts, 19, 72, 91-93, 121, 123, 127

H

heat pump, 64-66

heating systems, 11, 16, 58-71, 126
- central, 66
- forced air, 62-66
- heat pump, 64-66
- thermostat, 62-64

home inspection
- defined, 1-2, 6
- guarantee, 11-12
- limitations, 8, 12
- peace of mind, 3, 9, 15
- purpose, 1, 9, 15
- report, 7, 10, 11, 15, 16, 31, 129, 149-51
- standard operating procedures (SOP), 14

home inspector
- professional organizations, 6, 14, 149
  - American Society of Home Inspectors (ASHI), 6, 149, 152
  - International Association of Certified Home Inspectors (InterNACHI), 6
  - National Association of Home Inspectors (NAHI), 6, 153
- requirements, 6, 14
- selection, 6, 13, 14, 151

I

indoor air quality (IAQ), 37, 143-46

inspection

    types of

        air duct, 35

        annual maintenance, 32-33

        home energy audit, 34

        lead-based paint, 37

        mold testing, 36

        new homes, 7, 31

        pool and spa, 35

        pre-listing, 31-32

        radon and indoor air quality (IAQ), 37

        roof, 34-35

        septic system, 35

        sewer, 35

        special, 37

        termite, 34

        warranty, 30-31

        water quality testing, 36-37

International Association of Certified Home Inspectors (InterNACHI), 6

insects

    termites/wood-destroying, 7, 31, 73, 124, 131-34

insulation, 79, 94-98

    attic, 94, 97

    basement, 79

    R-value, 96-98

K

kitchen, 11, 26, 139

L

landscaping, 11

    decks, 139-41

    drainage, 75, 77, 106, 120-22

    foundation settlement, 75

    shrubs and trees, 123-26, 130

lead based paint, 37

M

maintenance, 1, 22, 24, 31, 32-33, 61, 71, 77, 82, 105, 126-28, 128, 129

mold, 36, 135-36

myths, 3-6

N

National Association of Home Inspectors (NAHI), 6, 153

P

peace of mind

    (see *home inspection, peace of mind*)

plumbing

    distribution piping, 17, 47, 50-52, 147

    galvanized pipes, 50-55

    leaks, 11, 24, 51, 53, 77, 127

    septic systems, 35, 56-58

    sink traps, 21, 24, 50

    toilets, 47-49

R

radon, 37

repair/remodeling

    (see *maintenance*)

report

    (see *home inspection, report*)

roofs, 11, 17, 18, 24, 27, 34-35, 82, 130

    flashing, 72, 85, 90-91, 128

    ice dam, 91-93

    metal, 85-87

    shingles, 87-89

    tile, 20, 82-85

    vents, 85, 95

S

safety glass, 108-10

septic tank, 56-58

shingles, 87-89

siding, 101-8
    aluminum, 72, 101-2
    masonry veneer, 105-8
    stucco, 104
    vinyl, 72, 102-3
    wood, 103-4

smoke detectors, 117, 143

staircase/steps, 11

stucco, 104

swamp cooler
    (see *air conditioning systems, evaporative cooler*)

T

termites, 7, 34, 76, 124, 131-34

thermostat, 62-64, 127

toilets, 47-48

trap, sink
    (see *plumbing, sink trap*)

V

vents

    air admittance valve (AAV), 19

    attic/roof, 84, 92, 95

    bathroom, 127

ventilation, 76-77, 94, 96

W

basement, 77, 78

exterior (see *siding*)

masonry, 105-7

siding (see *siding*)

veneer (see *siding*)

water stains, 107, 121, 125

waste water disposal

    septic system, 56-58

water

    contamination of, 19, 36-37

    ground (see *drainage*)

    leaking into attic, 27, 94

    seeping into basement, 75-76

water heater, 11, 17, 52-56, 127
  pressure/temperature relief valve (T&P valve), 21, 52-54
  relief valve, 52-54
  tank, 52, 55
  ventilation, 55
windows, 11, 108, 147
  egress, 110-13
  glass used in, 108-10
wood
  insects that destroy, 7, 34, 76, 125, 131-34
wood-burning stoves, 66, 68
  (see also *fireplaces*)

Y

yard
  (see *landscaping*)

About Frank Ross

Frank Ross is a serial entrepreneur and a dreamer at heart. His current project is building a home on a Caribbean island. Prior to retirement, Frank started and built up *Pillar to Post Home Inspection of Southwest Utah.* inspecting over 4200 homes. During his more than 13 years as a home inspector, he learned a thing or two about what buyers and homeowners need to know about homes and home inspection. In this latest book, Frank offers practical insights to home buyers and owners about the inspector's role in the home buying/selling process, maintaining a home's systems and how an inspection gives peace of mind. He is also the author of *A Frank Discussion About the Home Inspection Busines*s.

About Natalie Ross

Natalie Ross fills many roles: wife, mother, teacher, office manager, small business owner and mentor. Her educational background in Architecture and Design and decades of experience in various office environments qualify her to collaborate in making this dream book a reality. Natalie co-owned *Pillar to Post Home Inspection* and worked alongside Frank building up a successful enterprise. Without her leadership this book never would have made it past "That's a good idea."

www.ingramcontent.com/pod-product-compliance
Lightning Source LLC
Chambersburg PA
CBHW040328300426
44113CB00020B/2686